A Memoir by Stanley "Sonny" C

Whizzing Off tl

Stories of a World Champion F

Stan Sweet
White Sulphur Springs, West Virginia
June 2011

ACKNOWLEDGEMENTS

Many thanks go to my cousin, Jamie Cary of San Diego, California without whom I could not have put all these nutty things together for publication.

To my erudite niece, Chris Barbetti Feamster for her much needed help in the phrasing and verbiage of this entertainment piece.

Lastly a special thanks to Jamie's daughter-in-law, Julie Cary of Redlands, California for her artistic skills in designing and rendering the cover of this book.

PREFACE

My life has gone by at the speed of a fast draw. Just yesterday, it seems, I came kicking and screaming into this world, and now I'm the last surviving member of my family waiting to be planted in the earth. And the space between these two important events—well, that's what this book is all about: the eighty years of living that have come in between. My life has been outrageously funny, often zany, and frequently unpredictable, but it's always whizzed by at bullet speed.

I posed as a TV weatherman for over twenty-three years—it was a think-on-your-feet kind of a job back in the old days—but nothing could have prepared me for all the humor and oddity that I've encountered in my lifetime.

For as long as I can remember, I have loved the limelight. Hollywood was the place to be, and I couldn't wait to get there and make my mark. On my way to stardom, I took a few detours: college, the Army Air Corps, the altar, and several fast-draw championships, among others. These detours led me to countries all over the world, and every continent I traveled to had its own savory characters and stories.

I was also part of the early days of television, when anyone, and I mean anyone, could buy time on the air and create his own version of *Deal or No Deal*. There were no long, boring lines of credits at the end of my short-lived TV show. Heck, I didn't even know what a producer, director, or editor's job entailed. I just went out and found the advertising to pay for the air time. I dreamed up the program material, gathered all the props, and then bribed the guests to do whatever I wanted. No "reality" shows today could possibly rival all the drama, hilarity, and suspense that television offered with the unrehearsed live performances of the 1950s.

In the "Name Dropping" chapters, you'll find anecdotes and insights about famous people I've met along the way, including Clint Eastwood, Lucille Ball, Lilly Tomlin, Bob Denver, Oscar Levant, and many others who've sailed through my life. More importantly, you'll find out why it's imperative that you never stick your finger in a light socket while standing in water, as well as how to host a TV show and convince your guests to act like fools. If you read closely enough, you might even discover how to fake a fist fight or crack a twelve-foot bullwhip around your enemies before they know you're after them.

The following collection of short stories describes the people and animals I've met that left their mark on my life. Some of these tales are not for the faint of heart; the language is crude and the doings are coarse. But they are what they are: snippets of life at its rawest, of real people being real people. In other words, they're funny as hell!

If you think you're up to it, go take a whiz, plop down in your most comfortable lounge chair, and prepare for a rib-tickling, nostalgic trek into the past eighty years of a World Champion Fast-Draw TV Weatherman.

PART ONE:
ENTERTAINMENT ADVENTURES
AND
FAST-DRAW FUN

Chapter 1: The Fastest Gun Alive

A fast-draw-champion weatherman?" You may be asking. "How'd that happen?" Let me explain by starting my story right in the middle of things. In 1961 I was married with a family of my own and two stepchildren. At this point I was co-hosting an oddball sports program called Katzenjammer Sports on KTTV-TV in Hollywood. Unlike television today, we had no producers, directors, or multiple pages of credits to run following the program. My co-host Alton Tabor and I pretty much ran the whole show. Through various contacts I had developed by making commercials, I found sponsors who would pay for the air time. We saved lots of money by writing our own commercials and then acting in them. We purchased the cheapest time available from KTTV, which at that time was Sunday afternoon, and usually had enough funds left over to pay ourselves a modest salary.

Alton and I also rounded up the talent for Katzenjammer Sports. We invited sports enthusiasts of all kinds to visit the set and show films of their out-of-the-ordinary pursuits. The more dangerous the sport, the better the audience liked it. (It's pretty much the same way today.) We had skydiving experts whose motto was "the sky is my limit" and river busters who padded themselves up and swam downstream in rushing waters while bumping into boulders and logs. We once featured a one-seated gyrocopter demonstration. We also offered an archery exhibition—not to mention the one exhibition that changed the course of my life dramatically.

The Judge Colt Fast-Draw Club of Pomona, California came to our little show one day to perform some speedy Texas whip-outs. I was looking forward to this presentation—I had been known to play around with my little Mickey-Mouse Ruger .22 revolver, drawing it from a sloppy-flop holster. After the Judge Colt Fast-Draw Club's performance on our show (I helped with the demonstration as best I could as an untrained gunman), the members of the club, noting my keen interest in their art, invited me to come watch at their next practice. Of course I went—what red-white-and-blue-blooded American boy could pass up the lure of gunpowder and leather?

That did it. I was hooked for life. I joined their club, and every spare moment of my busy life I spent trying to become the fastest of them all.

 Many of these fast-draw competitions are held in the parking lots of hotels, malls, and car dealers, or just about anywhere someone will let us shoot. The main shooting area is always roped off with yellow police tape and monitored so no one from the crowd can enter and get hurt. Many different competitions take place at each meet, depending upon who is holding the event. One such competition is called an "elimination event." In an elimination event, your target is a steel silhouette fourteen inches wide and over thirty inches tall, with a three-inch-square chest-height cutout for a light. Heavy Plexiglas protects the light bulb and a microphone screwed onto the back of the silhouette receives the shock of the hit. A wire runs from the microphone to the timer clock, stopping it to record the first shot and its duration. For safety's sake, we use wax bullets propelled by pistol or shotgun primer caps. Large sheets of plywood provide backstops for the bullets in case a shooter's aim is a little off. At the end of the contest the

scores are added up, and the shooter with the lowest elapsed time wins. I like winning!

 In an actual Wild West shootout, there was no way to record how fast a shooter was. So, every time one cowboy challenged another to a shootout, he had no way of knowing whether he was faster or not until he was the one left standing. One of our competitions recreated the old-time western shootout.

Two shooters standing a hundred feet apart gradually start to walk toward each other. Both shooters' hands are near their Colt or Ruger single-action 45-caliber revolvers, which contain blank cartridges. The revolvers are snuggled in a holster hanging from a belt around the waist of either shooter. The shooters' eyes are intent on the signal light perched atop a tripod above a Chrondek timer clock. As the shooters reach the midway mark, the signal light flashes, and they draw and fire toward the clock and at each other. The sounds of the shots are picked up by microphones on either side of the clock. The lights on the clock show which shooter was the faster, and the Chrondek timer's sweep hand stops on the elapsed time in hundredths of a second. Hey, boys, is this fun, or what? Two wins out of three takes the round.

Eventually, fast-draw competitions evolved into variations on wax and blank shooting. The distances to the targets varied, and sometimes you had two targets to hit at once. In the "walk-and-draw level" competition, the loads were light, but when firing at balloons, heavy, dangerous blanks were fired—it takes large particles of gunpowder to pop balloons. When digital technology emerged, we began using electronic digital timers to time the draws. These were accurate to 1/1,000th of a second.

I created a makeshift practice range in my garage. I had my own fast-draw timer, and when I fired my primer caps, the sound was picked up by the microphone in the clock on the timer. It was hard work to polish my technique, learning to react quickly and hit the target accurately, but it paid off: in 1964 I placed in the top three in almost every local, regional, and national contest. After a couple more years of refining and quickening my draw, I went on to win two national championships and four world championships. The press dubbed me the "Fastest Gun Alive"—and I was, at least at that time. The sun doesn't shine on one dog's butt all the time, so even as a champion you know that honor may belong to someone else the next year. I enjoyed the title for as long as I had it and reveled in the accompanying fun.

The trophies kept collecting, so I decided to hold my own shootouts to get rid of them. I just removed the brass plates and presented them to the new winners of each competition. Yep, I probably won a lot more than my fair share of first-place trophies and the glory appertaining thereto. It was that glory as the fastest gun alive that led me into the next phase of my career, this time as a fast-draw comedian.

Chapter 2: South African
Fast-Draw Comedy Tour

If there were anything funny about shooting a gun, the trickster-clown in me could find it. As my repertoire of gun tricks grew, so did my audiences, until one day someone offered to pay me for doing my comedy routine.

Hot diggity! Getting paid to have fun was my kind of job. The most famous western characters on the silver screen and TV at that time included greats like John Wayne, James Arness, Walter Brennan, and Dan Blocker. In my routine, I made fun of these Hollywood idols by mimicking their voices and performing tricky gun-handling feats—firing, of course, only blank cartridges. Audiences loved the humor, along with all the antics I had the slow-drawing characters perform. The more I performed the more bookings I received.

The National School Assemblies Agency in North Hollywood heard about my comedy gun routine and offered to represent me in booking my show across an eleven-state area. Gee! At that time I was only doing about fifteen bookings a year, working them in between my jobs as a house painter. (Yeah, I was painting houses. Show biz is pretty unstable.) I was flattered, but when I found out they wanted a thirty percent commission, I almost fell over—that was three times the normal agent's fee. I turned them down.

Bad move. My bookings had always come from word-of-mouth referrals, and the next year I had only a few gigs. Phooey.

The next year I decided to go ahead and sign up with the agency. I swallowed hard and paid the thirty percent fee—fifteen percent to their field salesman and fifteen percent to the agency itself. All they asked me was how much I wanted to net; then they added their thirty percent to the total offered to the group hosting the show. Simple, huh? Duh. Why hadn't I thought of that before? Why hadn't I asked more questions? I finally realized that I didn't care how much the agency made, as long as I got the fee I needed. That little lesson cost me a lot of money, but I never forgot it. It reminds me of a sign I once saw in a factory that said, "Thimk before you louse it up." I always try to "thimk" first nowadays.

Once I was signed on with the National School Assemblies Agency, I appeared at colleges and high schools, and sometimes at grade-school assemblies, in California, Utah, Colorado, Arizona, New Mexico, and

Washington. But my most memorable experience as a gun-toting fast-draw entertainer came in the summer of 1973. I had some free time on my hands because the painting business was about as slow as show biz, so my regular talent agent, Eddie Cochran of Hollywood, booked me on a six-month tour of South Africa with a large variety show called The Minstrel Follies. The booking took me on a whirlwind tour of Cape Town, Pretoria, Durban, and Johannesburg. When we landed in Cape Town, the stewardess on the plane told us to set our watches back thirty years.

It's probably hard to believe, but back in the early 1970s there was no television in South Africa, so live entertainment was very popular with the townspeople. The Minstrel Follies (not The "Menstrual" Follies, as some insisted on calling us) was a high-class production that included a British stand-up comic as the master of ceremonies, a French acrobatic team, an Italian clown group, lots of talented singers and dancers, and *me*, the U.S. National Fast-Draw Champion. We were a politically correct, international bunch! My complete comedy gun routine lasted a healthy eleven minutes, which was the most stage time given to any of the performers. When the routine went well, that eleven minutes went fast—but when the audience was too sophisticated for my dumb cowboy antics, I couldn't get off that stage quickly enough.

British emcee Derek Dene also spent a great deal of time on stage telling jokes. His favorite crack was about visiting London and going to his first topless restaurant. "The sign outside said 'topless restaurant,' so I thought I'd try it," he told the audience. "I knew that most claims of this nature were exaggerated, but I went inside this place anyway. And sure enough, it was a topless restaurant, because it had no roof! It was pouring down rain, and it took me a half hour to finish my soup." The audience loved that one.

Another story Derek liked to tell was about his first trip to Africa. "Everyone dresses differently here," he explained. "But one day I was in a restroom and I saw a man dressed like I was dressed. He was standing in front of the lavatory trying to get some food grease off his hands. Aha! I said to this fellow, 'European?' 'No, no,' said the fellow, 'I'm just washing my hands.'"

Sometimes it took the audience a while to get that one.

Derek could keep 'em coming. "I was up on the roof of the tallest building in Cape Town the other day," he'd say. "It was breathtaking! But I was scared to say 'My God,' lest I get an answer." Derek Dene was a laugh machine.

In 1973 there were no equal rights in South Africa. Our shows were exclusively for whites, with the exception of one performance in Durban, where they permitted Niet Blancs (Non-Whites), or, in this case, those who were not considered white, but were East Indian or Japanese. (The Chinese were not included in this assemblage, but the Japanese, who did a lot of business with South Africans, were. Go figure.)

Looking out across this group, an exception to South Africa's normally strict code of discrimination, I saw the most lavishly dressed people I'd ever seen, especially the East Indians, who made up a huge colony in this thriving city. (Durban was at that time the Miami Beach of South Africa.) They had on gorgeous gowns and dresses, with flashy jewelry that positively dazzled the beholder.

They also laughed at things in my show that didn't normally get laughs, and stayed quiet for some of my best stuff that always got a good rise out of the audience. One typical bit was where I'd pick up the two guns and say, "I guess you're all wondering why *this* gun looks bigger than the other one." Then, a heartbeat later, I'd say, "That's because of its size." With this crowd, it went over like a clod of dirt in a punch bowl. They did laugh when I imitated the voices of Hoss Cartwright, John Wayne, and Walter Brennan. They must have seen a lot of American movies. All in all, though, they were a decent audience—everyone had fun.

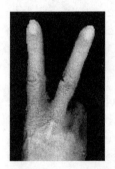 In my fast-draw routine, I would draw the old Colt .45 from the fancy holster and fire two shots so fast that they sounded like just one shot. Then I would prove that I had fired two by moving the gun downward very fast as I fired the two shots again, making two flashes that verified my claim. I would fire three in a row to sound like a machine gun, and then ask the folks to get ready and clap their hands fast when they saw me go for the gun on the next draw. I would warn them to be ready, then draw and fire a blank cartridge before they could sound their hands together. BANG! CLAP! Too late, folks.

Even though most everyone spoke English, some English words have a different meaning in South Africa. In my show I'd draw, fire, and put the gun back in the holster so fast you couldn't believe your eyes. Once, after doing this trick, I said, "Tricky, huh? Like a pair of rubber crutches." When I got backstage I was told that "crutch" meant "crotch" in South African English, and that people would wonder what "rubber crotches" were. Once, after a show, I said out loud to the assemblage backstage, "Well, I'd better get my fanny in gear and go up and wash some things out in the lavatory." What I had said, as far as they were concerned, was, "I'd better get my vagina in gear and go wash some things out in the toilet." Oh, boy.

Let's go back to the double shots that sounded as one. Here was another fine faux pas you got yourself into, Stanley. When I had proven my case with the two shots, I held up two fingers to reinforce my declaration, saying, "That's *two*, two shots."

Now, we all know that, in America, shoving your middle finger into the air constitutes a rude gesture, meaning "up yours." But holding up two fingers certainly couldn't have an impolite or sexual connotation, right? Wrong. In Britain, South Africa, and Australia, it denotes the same thing as our raised middle digit, as if to say to someone, "Twirl, squirrel."

This I did not know until I got backstage, where the producer and the other cast members were laughing at me. "You just now gave the audience 'the shaft,' Stan," they explained to me between guffaws. Was I ever embarrassed! Durn these "foreigners" and their weird customs.

In one of my other bits, I'd put an empty tin can in the jaws of a C clamp, hold it up toward backstage, and fire a big, "harmless" blank into it at point-blank range. The shot produced a huge, gaping hole, showing the audience how dangerous a "harmless" blank could be. One night, the psychic Uri Geller was taking in our show, sitting back in the fourth row. A tiny fragment of the tin can must have bounced backward into the audience, because it hit him on the cheek and made a tiny nick. That was the last time I used the tin can; nevertheless, Uri was a good sport. He came up on stage after the show, shook my hand, told me about it, and demonstrated some of his own stunts.

We were all fascinated by his bending of spoons and keys, not to mention his mindreading. That night he asked for a volunteer, and a young dancer came forward. He asked her to draw a simple object while his back was turned, to see if he could read her mind. He put his hands over his eyes and turned away while she drew a crude sketch of a pine tree, then put the drawing behind her back and told him she was ready. He looked at her and asked her to draw the picture in her mind several times. Then he took another piece of paper and drew another pine tree, much like hers. We were all amazed—we'd been watching carefully to see if he was fudging.

Then he looked puzzled and asked her if she had thought of something else before she drew the tree. She apologized shyly and told him that she had started to draw something else, but didn't think she could do it justice. Uri knocked us all for a loop when he asked her if it happened to be a pussycat, and she said yes. She was doubly amazed, just like the rest of us, at his mysterious talent.

Uri and about ten of us performers were sitting around in one of our hotel rooms after the show, where he would bend keys for us by gently caressing them with forefinger and thumb until they began to arch. Weird. Then he asked me if I wanted him to read my mind. I nodded. He turned around so he couldn't see what I was drawing. Since his manager was standing in the group, I cupped my left hand around the pen and moved it so that he couldn't tell which way the pen was going, either. I drew some railroad tracks, like these:

I made two straight lines, left to right, then made lines crossing the "rails" to resemble railroad ties. Then I turned the paper over and told him I was ready. He turned to face me and asked me to draw the same thing in my mind's eye a few times. I did. Then he took a piece of paper and drew two horizontal lines, just like mine. Down lower, not quite crossing them like I had, he drew the "ties." He looked perplexed, wondering what I had drawn.

I explained what it was, showing him my slightly different drawing—but we were all still amazed that he really could approximate what I had sketched.

Uri wanted to examine one of my Colt .45s, but my girlfriend, Heather Wren, advised against it, worried that he might bend the barrel and make it shoot crooked—she *really* believed. (This was, remember, back in the early 1970s. Heather asked me to be sure to describe her to my folks at home as an English-speaking, *white* South African.)

Later I helped Uri Geller find a gun for personal protection by taking him to a gun shop, where he selected a small Beretta 25-caliber semiautomatic pistol. The employees and customers already had heard about his key-bending feats, and several of them wanted one bent for a souvenir, so he accommodated them on the spot. One guy said that one of the keys in his pocket had bent on its own while Uri was bending another key. I was carrying my old apartment key, so I joined the others and got him to bend it for my son, Dana. I honestly couldn't bend it the normal way, with my bare fingers. Uri had a number of his own performances booked in the same city, so we didn't see much more of him, but we were all believers, I can tell you that.

Backstage, before, during, and after a performance, the dancing girls were always in various modes of dress and undress, and the stage manager was very careful that none of our black South African helpers were allowed to see them showing too much skin. Some of the more curvaceous gals, though, were stationed on stage during a skit, wearing nothing on top but pasties over their nipples. They were not allowed to move a muscle—they stood there motionless while the slimmer gals danced. The fear was that, if they moved, their breasts would jiggle seductively, sensationalizing the performance more than was discreet or decent. Yeah, right.

Offstage and walking around the cities we visited, I always carried one of my Colts tucked into my waist, so that if someone broke into my hotel room and stole my other guns I wouldn't be completely out of business. I carried it with the hammer down on an empty chamber and five "harmful" blanks in the others. The thinking was that, no matter how big an attacker was, I could push the gun into his gut and blow a big chunk of him away. Yes, it sounds terrible, but I was in a foreign country and felt that I needed protection. I never did, though.

The law allowed me to carry a gun, but I was required to cover it so it couldn't be seen, so I wore a light jacket or a sweater. One male dancer of questionable masculinity asked me if he could feel how hard the gun was, but I smiled and turned him down.

"You must think I'm gay," he said. "I'm really not, but my boyfriend is."

I smiled again and said, "That's an oldie, but a goodie."

While I was living in South Africa (the tour lasted six months), the Watergate scandal erupted. Curious residents asked how I felt about the mess. I said, "I'm very proud to be from a country that is truly run by the people—and where, if even the very top man of the land violates the law, he can and will be brought down from his lofty perch to answer to us common citizens. You don't need to use all the fingers on one hand to count the countries where this could happen. Isn't that fantastic?" They didn't know what to say—they had thought I'd be ashamed.

One day while we were in Johannesburg, we got our regular two-day break in the action and Heather suggested we visit a wild animal game reserve nearby. It sounded like a winning proposition, so we packed up for a trip into the hinterlands to what was called a "giraffe farm." They had all kinds of wild animals on the farm, so I wondered why they called it by just one animal's name.

 There was a baboon in a steel cage. They pronounced "baboon" with the accent on the last syllable, "buh-BOON," so they called him "P-Pat B-Boone." I looked at him with a studied, curious interest, and he flat-out went wild, screeching and carrying on like a nut. Heather, no stranger to the local wild animals, told me *never* to stare at baboons—they

take it as a challenge and will tear you apart if they're free. Good grief! Touchy devils, aren't they?

That baboon reminded me of the time I was touring Northern California near Salinas with my fast-gun show. At the Salinas County Fair, where we were performing, a big, black female panther was kept backstage in a steel-barred cage. I was standing six or seven yards from the front of the cage when the animal trainer, a tough-looking gal who looked like a hangover from a wrong decision, told me to be sure not to stand too close to the big cat. Why?

"Because she might try to pee on you," she said.

I couldn't figure out how that could affect me, as far away as I was. But a few minutes later, this huge cat turned around backwards, put her butt up against the bars, and shot a stream of urine over twenty feet. It landed just in front of me. Whew! I believed the keeper then, and kept a much greater distance from this overgrown pussycat.

Ian MacDonald, the manager of the giraffe farm that Heather and I were visiting, was a nice guy who bent over backwards to make our short stay a pleasant one. He had a couple of whites and about fifteen blacks helping him run the place. I had my guns and ammo with me, so I did a brief fast-gun demonstration for them in front of their offices. They were all taken aback by my dexterity and looked up to me as one really macho fellow.

That night in our cabin we could hear a loud chorus of animals roaring and screaming at one another. The hyenas, with their screechy laughs, were the worst; they didn't allow us much sleep.

The next day we were talking with Ian about the superstitions of the "Kaffirs" who worked for him. "Kaffir" was a derogatory term used by South Africans to describe the natives who were fresh from the outlying bush or countryside and weren't "civilized" like their counterparts in the big cities. They also used the term to express general derision.

 Anyway, Ian had a glass eye, which he would take out, wash off, and replace now and then when it was hurting his eye socket. He told us a story about how superstitious his work crew was. His glass eye was irritating him one day, so he took it out to give his socket some rest. As he was trying to put it into his pocket, he dropped it without knowing it. It fell into the dirt, and he continued without realizing what had happened. When he reached a water fountain for a drink, he reached into his pocket for the eye so he could wash and replace it, but it was missing. He told the workers about his loss and asked them to keep an "eye" out for it.

Two days later, one of his black helpers strode up to him, sidling like a sidewinder and holding his hand out. His fist was closed, with a finger pointing to the ground. He seemed embarrassed as he approached Ian and said simply, "For you, sir." MacDonald held his open palm under the man's hand, and the man deposited the glass eye into it. It was covered with dirt. The fellow seemed ashamed and afraid and spun on his heels, retreating to join the others without another word.

On another occasion he had a bunch of men working on a fence and clearing brush about twenty minutes away from the offices. He received a radio call asking him to hurry back to the office to straighten out an emergency situation. The men were clearing brush at the time, but he suspected that if he left them they'd plop down and loaf while he was gone. He took out his glass eye and placed it atop a post as if to watch them, then jumped into his Jeep to sort things out at headquarters.

When Ian came back a half hour later, he found them all loafing and piddling around. Seeing him arrive, they hurried back to their jobs. He glanced at the post that held his glass eye. A hat was covering it. (Obviously, one of them had sneaked around behind it and dropped a hat over it to keep it from seeing what they weren't doing.) Ian put it down to "Kaffir logic."

On our second day at the giraffe farm, Heather and I accompanied Ian into the bush to check on some mysterious spoor (animal tracks). They were both leaning over, checking out some large foot or paw prints, when we heard a soft but clear "*HARUMPH!*" over the small knoll to our left. Heather, no bush neophyte, claimed that it was the unmistakable sound of a large male lion. Ian agreed, but seemed unperturbed. Since they wanted to follow the tracks into the brush to our right, he handed me his .357 magnum revolver. He asked me not to shoot if the lion popped up over the knoll to our left and didn't threaten us. But, he said, if the animal started charging me, I was to wait until it was in range and then cut loose with everything I had.

Oh, boy. "Great!" I thought as I hefted the heavy gun. "I can just see the headlines: 'Skittish American Slaughters Tame Park Lion.' Or, worse yet: 'American Mauled After Shooting and Angering Park Lion.'" Luckily, we didn't actually see any wild animals in that particular locale.

These are just a few memories from my six-month tour of South Africa. I enjoyed almost every minute of it, but I was delighted to get back to the good old U.S. of A.

Chapter 3: Hollywood Stunt Work

They do an awful lot of faking in Hollywood. Well, *some* of it is awful, but most of it is very good.

Come on, now—if you see a body falling out of a twenty-story building and bouncing on the cement below, you *know* it's not a real person. It's a dummy. You'd *have* to be a dummy to take a job like that. Everyone already knows why they have to fake it—to preserve human life and health, not to mention expensive property.

Let's face it. You can't just manufacture a real earthquake whenever you want it, or crash a real airplane into a hillside in order to film a good sequence. They have to use models or digital recreations or some other fabrication to produce the illusion for you.

The first brush I ever had with stunt work was when I was in basic training for the Army Air Corps. A whole gang of us trainees happened to be just outside the barracks one afternoon, waiting for the mess call, when two fellows got into a fistfight. We backed off, giving them room to have it out, and made a big circle around them as an impromptu audience. Eventually, one of them was knocked to the ground, and the one left standing started to kick the poor guy who was down.

You could hear the loser of the battle grunt in pain as the other one hauled off and kicked the tar out of him. A couple of the onlookers yelled "Hey!" but nobody else appeared to care that this display was unfair and hurtful.

25

It angered me to such an extent that I stepped forward and told the guy to stop it, in no uncertain terms. To my surprise, he didn't threaten me as I had thought he would. Instead, the bizarre next moment left us all flabbergasted: the guy on the ground jumped up and patted his opponent on the back. Then they both started laughing like hyenas. They explained that they were, in fact, Hollywood stuntmen, just messing around to see if they could fool us. They showed us how one of them would hold an open palm up under his chin while the other fighter would swing his fist into that hand. The hit to the hand would make a loud smack; meanwhile, the receiver would snap his head to make it look as if he had been hit on the chin.

As far as the kicking was concerned, the one on the ground would arch his body to make room for the kicker's instep; meanwhile, the kicker would pull his kick so that it only *looked* swift and hard. The grounded fighter would grunt and arch up in the air as if the kick were knocking him along. Their live sound effects wouldn't be needed when filming a movie, they told us, because the grunting, chin hits, and other sound effects would be dubbed into the film in the editing room. We were amazed at these revelations of Hollywood trickery and joined in with the laughter.

Almost twenty years later I met another stuntman, Monty Laird, who attended one of our fast-draw competitions to study our techniques. He was impressed with our obvious superiority in drawing and shooting, and we became good friends. Monty had small acting roles in many motion pictures and was a stand-in for actor Pete Duel while they were filming the *Alias Smith*

& *Jones* TV series at the ABC studios. He didn't look anything like Duel, but supplied the body of a similarly built man as they blocked out their moves and placed the set lighting.

It wasn't exactly stunt work, but it kept Monty busy earning a decent living in the TV and movie business. Pete Duel and Ben Murphy had a successful run with this series in 1971, but Duel committed suicide on the last day of the year. They say he suffered from depression and alcohol addiction.

Monty taught me how to crack a twelve-foot bullwhip around a person without hurting the "whippee." He also showed me how to manage fake fistfights, which I started using in my fast-draw comedy routines.

When I made stage presentations to colleges, I chose a couple of fearless young men before the show started, then rehearsed with them in an empty side room so the audience wouldn't know what tricks were coming. For the young fellow who was to be "whipped," I would take a red felt pen, lift up his T-shirt, and rake a red stripe across his stomach, then let his shirt back down. While no one could witness it, I'd coach him on how to react. I would set this up later by telling the audience that I could snap the whip around the lad without even hurting him. To make them worry, I would say I had "just learned this trick yesterday." On stage, I would crack the whip about three feet past him, letting it wrap his midsection so that it gave the impression that the crack of the whip had hit his body. He would grimace, say "Ouch," rub his belly, and give me a dirty look.

"How many of you think I really hurt him just then?" I'd ask. Most would raise their hands. Then I'd pull up his shirttail without appearing to notice the felt pen mark and say, "Look, it didn't even leave a mark!" Of course, they would see the "welt" that the whip had purportedly made, feel sorry for the poor guy, and wonder if I'd lost my marbles. Then I'd explain that it was just a gag, that it hadn't hurt him at all, and that I had used a red felt pen to make the mark.

For the fistfight routines I would place one of my "stuntmen" upstage from me, so the folks couldn't see how far I was missing him with my "hits." He would take a swing at me; I'd block it with my left arm, then pretend to hit him in the gut. He'd grunt and bend over in "pain," and I'd uppercut him to the floor. Taking a cue from the Air Corps boys, I'd pretend-kick him, and he'd grunt and act as if he were lifted along by my blows.

That fellow would say, "I'll get even with you," then go offstage to get ready for the next bit of action. First I'd pretend to talk with some lady about the weather. Then a plant in the front row would yell, "Look out. He's got a gun!" That was my cue to whirl around, then draw and fire a blank at my gun-pointing stunt helper, who would be standing to the far left upstage. He would grab his stomach and bend over, but would keep lurching toward me. I'd tell him to go on home before it got worse, but he would start to raise the gun again at me, so I'd shoot him in the left shoulder. He'd spin that shoulder around and fall to the floor. I'd re-holster the gun as if that were it.

As if resuming my chat with my imaginary lady friend, I'd say, "Sorry, ma'am. Before I was so rudely interrupted . . ."

At that moment the guy on the floor would aim his gun at my back. My audience plant would yell again, "Look out!" That was my cue to cut loose and fire four more blanks at him, watching him jerk and roll away as each shot rang out. The audience knew we were faking, but it had enough dramatic realism to it to create some suspense and doubt.

One time Monty and a stuntman friend offered to help me spice up my comedy act—and, of course, show off a little. The event was a high school assembly in the San Fernando Valley. It was held in the gymnasium; all the faculty and students sat on one side of the gym, and the bleachers on the opposite side were empty—almost. Monty's buddy was standing at the top of the aisle, yelling and pointing a phony gun at me. I drew and fired, then we watched this guy clutch his gut, fall, and roll down every one of those bone-breakingly hard steps, clunking the whole way, and land in a heap at the bottom. These men were tough as nails.

Before you could say "Jack Robinson," Monty yelled out from the top of a basketball hoop, waving a fake rubber gun at me. I drew and fired one shot at him, but he opened his legs wide (as if the bullet had gone through them), laughed, and said, "Ha, ha. You missed me." Then I shot two more blanks at him. He grabbed his chest, lurched backwards a little, plummeted down from his perch, did a half flip, and landed flat on his back on a pile of wrestling mats.

The art of it was to land flat enough to distribute the weight of the long fall. If you landed on your feet, you'd drive your knees up around your shoulders. If you landed on your head, you wouldn't be able to close your shirt collar again, your neck would be so squashed. The school group was so impressed with their performances that when I introduced them again, complimented them, and asked for a hand, the standing ovation lasted over half a minute.

During one live stunt show in the Valley, Monty got his knuckles stomped on so hard that it broke bones and brought tears to his eyes, but he carried on with a smile until the finish. Another time, at one of the big Las Vegas nightclubs, they did all sorts of live stunts, finishing with his crash through a railing and fall from the upstairs balcony. He landed on a breakaway balsa wood table that had springs to soften the fall, but he landed wrong. It hurt like the devil—in fact, it was so excruciating that he could barely walk when it came time to leave the stage. When he got outside, he screamed at the top of his lungs. It almost stopped traffic, it was so loud. What a trouper!

I've come to a conclusion concerning the rough-and-tumble job of a stuntman: that type of work is positively *not* the career I'd ever choose.

The following year, they started filming the *Beretta* TV series at one of the studios. Monty invited me to watch them film the first scenes of the pilot episode. For about twenty minutes, everything went very well. Then Robert Blake, the star of the series, blew one of his lines and became angry. Blaming it on those of us who were standing around watching, he demanded that anyone not involved in the actual shooting of the scene leave the set—so we did. It sure smacked of pettiness on Blake's part, but we were in no position to argue.

A few years later, on the *Johnny Carson Show*, Robert Blake confessed to being capricious and high-strung. He admitted that he, himself, had been kicked off of a movie set. "Well, good for him," I thought.

Chapter 4: Name Dropping

While working at TV stations, filming TV commercials in Hollywood for Parkway Ford in Pasadena, appearing here and there as the World's Overall Fast-Draw Champion, or doing gun demonstrations, I interviewed, talked with, and met a lot of famous and semi-famous people.

In the 1950s I was a staff announcer for WSAZ-TV in Huntington, West Virginia. One day, glitzy pianist Liberace came to town for a concert.

To enhance his publicity and build some extra hype, he visited our studios. In those days we didn't have tapes with picture and sound, so they wanted some silent film of this great man shaking hands with a few of us common folk. I must have had a serious look on my face when I shook his hand, because Liberace said to me, "Smile, Stan. People who meet Liberace are very happy." Of course, of course—I complied and smiled broadly for the camera. No need to spoil his image.

Country crooner Eddie Arnold was not as particular, so when he came to the studios, all I had to do was shake his hand. I noticed that he had big, rough farmer's hands. Well, isn't that why they called him "The Tennessee Plowboy?"

Speaking of hands, when Bob Barker and I met and shook hands on his Truth or Consequences program, I noticed that he had a very long, slim hand, like a female pianist. On his show I had my two-foot, square-faced fast-draw timer that told you who had fired first when two competitors shot it out. The clock also had a sweep hand that indicated how much of one second it took for the winner to fire that shot.

Bob's producers came up with a bit in which two women from the audience were each handed one of my Colt .45 revolvers, loaded with small blank cartridges. The women stood a few feet back on either side of the clock and were told that, when the starting light turned on and after I gave the "ready" signal, they were to fire their already-cocked pistols at the clock. A light on the winner's side would announce her victory. The fastest drawer won an expensive home appliance. I ran the contest after being introduced as the World's Fast-Draw Champion.

One day, Larry Sutton, a friend and co-worker at Maywood Bell Ford in Los Angeles, where I sold cars and pickup trucks, invited my wife and me to a spaghetti dinner at his home in Studio City, just north of Hollywood. Also at the table were Larry's wife, a guy by the name of Clint Eastwood, and his wife. Clint told us that he had been working at a gas station when the famous Eddie Cantor came by and got him a screen test at one of the studios.

We all acknowledged his good fortune and wished him luck. That was the end of the matter: we said our goodbyes, and I didn't hear anything about Larry or Clint for a year or more.

A Western series called Rawhide was on the television in our front room one night when my wife exclaimed, "Look, there's Clint Eastwood!"

I said, "Who's Clint Eastwood?"

Then she reminded me of our dinner with Larry.

I said, "Oh, yeah. Well, he got a job. Good for him." Little did we know how many jobs he would get later on.

Rawhide became a very popular series. When I was in Las Vegas, shooting in a big strip hotel arena for the world championships, I saw several of the cast mingling with the crowd, signing autographs. Among them were Paul Brinegar (Wishbone), Eric Fleming (Gil Favor), and our boy, Clint Eastwood (Rowdy Yates). Sitting alongside me in the arena was a young gal shooter, who mentioned that she'd love to have Clint's autograph, but was too shy to ask him. So I told her the circumstances of my meeting him and offered to go get the autograph.

I approached "Rowdy Yates" with a pen and piece of paper, reminded him of our meeting in Studio City, and asked him if he'd heard anything from Larry Sutton lately. He acknowledged our meeting cordially and told me he'd never heard a word from Larry in all this time. He signed the paper, and that was the last personal contact I had with the guy. Not everyone loved him: some people said he had just two poses: one where he squints and one where he doesn't. At any rate, he went on to become one of the biggest stars Hollywood has ever seen.

Also appearing on the scene during our breaks from the shooting contest was Paramount Studios' gun coach, Rodd Redwing. Rodd was a full-blooded Indian who appeared in many Westerns. He also demonstrated expert gun handling.

Rodd would stand about twenty feet back from a stand that held a steel-lined foot-square shadow box holding a white sugar wafer about the size of a quarter glued to its center with nothing but spit. The wafer was about waist high, and Rodd would surreptitiously take the heel of his right hand and cock the pistol just before he drew and shot. (We shooters noticed this bit of an edge he took, but no one else did.)

Then he would draw the gun and shoot 22-caliber gallery short slugs (frangibles) at the wafer, the bullet shattering as it hit anywhere in the box, splattering the wafer into fine powder. It was dramatic—a nice bit of deception—and it amazed the audience. He performed some other feats of expertise and talked with a few of us gunslingers after his show, letting us take a look at his gear. When Rodd died a couple of years later, our holster maker, Alfonso Piñeda, asked me to appear on TV to sing his praises in a special salute to this fine gunman-actor.

I mention Robert Horton of the Wagon Train TV series only in passing. He awarded me my trophy at the fast-draw contest at the Clam Festival in Pismo Beach, California. The trophy was for winning the fastest double-balloon target series. I didn't manage to win the overall prize that day. Tough luck.

While I'm mentioning my brushes with celebrity, I have to say something about Johnny Olson, famous mostly as the resident announcer on The Price Is Right. If you'll remember, he was the loud-and-clear voice yelling "Come on down!" to the contestant who had just been chosen to guess prices on the program.

Johnny had a wife and home in Lewisburg, West Virginia, just ten miles away from my hometown, where I was a disc jockey on WSLW Radio. He didn't have a very deep voice, but it was pleasantly clear—it commanded your attention. He appeared on my pop-music show occasionally, and I used to ask him all about Hollywood. He also recorded some great promos for the station as a courtesy. One of them was, "You're within the giant reach of WSLW radio, White Sulphur-Lewisburg!"

The last time I saw Johnny was at CBS Television City in West Los Angeles, where my daughter Caroline and I visited the set of The Price Is Right as his guests and had our picture taken with him. The Lord only knows where that picture is now.

Ralph Edwards hosted several game shows. Of greatest note was the popular This Is Your Life, in which he'd surprise celebrities in the audience by bringing them up on stage and parading their old friends and relatives onto the scene, condensing the highlights of the subjects' lives into the time allotted.

When Ralph was the host of Truth or Consequences he convinced the residents of a town in New Mexico to change the name of their town to the name of his show. To seal the deal, he promised them he would bring in a troupe of entertainers once a year for a specified term of years. It was a blatant publicity stunt, but his producers and the residents were happy about all the exposure—not to mention the complimentary fun the residents enjoyed for a day or so each year.

In 1972 my agent booked me and my fast-draw comedy act with this yearly group as another entertainer for their stage performances. Also appearing were celebrities like Dick Contino, the then-famous "Lady of Spain" accordionist; Sue Ane Langdon, popular movie and TV actress; and Pat Buttram, sidekick to singing cowboy stars and others. Pat Buttram did a fabulous stand-up comedy routine that included remarks like "Things are really different for short-short people. They're the last to know when it rains and things smell different to very short people. Take, for instance, in a crowded elevator."

Pat played the part of Mr. Haney on the long-running comedy series Green Acres. He was the one with the high voice, and certainly did his part to garner laughs in the studio. He told me that he once offered Gene Autry a gag to use when people asked why he wore two guns. He suggested that Gene say, "One gun won't shoot far enough." He also suggested that Gene should threaten bad guys with, "I'll pump so much lead in your butt, when you 'set' down, you'll leave pencil marks." Gene didn't buy either bit, but I said maybe I could incorporate them into my gun show and give him credit for it. (He said I didn't need to mention him.) He even wrote a poem: "Backward, fly backward, O time in thy flight; I've thought of a comeback I needed last night." He was a clever, funny guy in person, but nothing like the characters he played in the movies and on TV.

In Camden Park, near Huntington, West Virginia, I covered an interview with their stage performer for the TV station. They called him "Ukulele Ike," but his real name was Cliff Edwards. He did a fine stand-up routine on stage, wisecracking and playing the ukulele, singing hit songs from his movie appearances.

Cliff was the voice of Jiminy Cricket in Disney's animated film Pinocchio. He sang "When You Wish Upon a Star," which became a big commercial hit. He did a fantastic job, but little did the audience know that he always had a snoot full before he went on stage. He was drunk as a monkey, but once he was on stage, you'd never know it. What a performer!

 One of the producers of Pat Robertson's 700 Club found out about my comedy gun show and asked me to appear on the program to perform. This was a big departure from their usual religious programming, but it all went well. Danuta Soderman, a cohost at the time, slapped on a gun and holster to join in the spirit of the show. One of my stunts was to draw and fire all six blanks in less than one

second. When the smoke cleared, Danuta was cringing and holding her ears. The audience ate up my comedic patter and a jolly time was had by all. Later I tape-recorded an interview with Pat for broadcast at our local radio station.

We held some of our smaller fast-draw contests in Glendora, California, a suburb of Los Angeles. Movie actor Woody Strode showed up from time to time to watch our fast-gun activities. Though he was black, he portrayed Native Americans (called "Indians" back then) in Westerns.

Woody lived on the hill just above Glendora with his Hawaiian wife, Luukialuana, whom he called "Mama." We'd listen to him tell stories about events during scene shoots for movies such as The Professionals. He had such an interesting face and strong build that he graced many Western movie sets in those days. Woody just laughed when I told him that, in one of the outdoor scenes in The Professionals, if you looked past Burt Lancaster and to the right you could see a horse taking a dump about thirty yards behind the actors. "They left it in on purpose," he told me.

Back in the late 1950s I used to drive from one TV station to the other in Hollywood, doing commercials for Parkway Ford in Pasadena. When the salesmen there closed a deal, they were to ask how the person knew about us. This was called "sourcing," and the most popular source was a talk show hosted by one Tom Duggan. I appeared on his show with our commercials.

Now, Tom was a sharp-tongued interviewer of movie and TV stars, so when my turn came to do a 90-second commercial, he would interrupt me several times in that supposed minute and a half. He'd make witty remarks, ask embarrassing questions (which got a lot of laughs from the studio audience) and sometimes extend my time on the air to well over two minutes. I was an ideal foil for his "Tomfoolery," which broke me up no end. Those commercials went over big at the car dealership—not only did they garner more air time, but they also pleased the viewers and sold us a lot of cars and trucks.

Lucille Ball and William Frawley of I Love Lucy visited Tom Duggan's set one evening for interviews. We were all in the green room when Lucy came to me and said, "I know you. You do the car commercials that Tom won't let you finish." Well, that was a great boost to my ego, to be recognized by this famous lady! I asked her a few questions before the show and noticed that the skin on her face was full of tiny, tiny cracks, no doubt from all the makeup she'd worn through the years. I wondered how they would show up on TV when Tom interviewed her. Somebody must have gotten the word somehow, because the cameraman backed off on his sharpest focus and you couldn't tell at all. Clever.

Parkway Ford also sponsored the showing of old movies on KABC-TV. I hosted them, announcing commercials during the breaks. One day character actor and movie star Lee Van Cleef came to the set, right out of the blue. I don't know why he was there, but I took the opportunity and asked him to do a quick skit with me during one of the commercial breaks. I had on my cowboy gun and rig for the Western movie, so I proposed that we shoot it out with blanks. He borrowed one of my guns and we had at it. I let the bad guy win for a change and fell over in a heap.

Most people didn't know that Lee was a serious photographer. He even gave me a business card touting him as a bona fide commercial picture taker. How about that?

Along about that same time, character actor and occasional movie lead Aldo Ray dropped into the studios where I hosted the old movies. After I interviewed him, we enjoyed a drink in a nearby bar.

Among other things Aldo told me about his career, he confessed that he had a big, fat crush on Tina Louise—Ginger of Gilligan's Island fame. From what I heard, he was lucky he didn't tie up with such a high-strung gal.

41

How about Oscar Levant? Young folks have probably never heard of him, but he was a big name at one time. Oscar was famous for his pianistic prowess and movie acting. He specialized in George Gershwin melodies, especially "Rhapsody in Blue," a brilliant composition I have always enjoyed.

Oscar was a self-proclaimed genius with a dry wit. He had his own local talk show on TV at one of the Hollywood studios; I did my car commercials on the show once in a while. He had an acid tongue—once, after I'd read an Old Gold Cigarette commercial, he remarked with a smirk as I sat beside him that I was "soporific" (sleep-inducing).

He asked me, "You know what 'soporific' means, don't you?"

"Yes," I said, "but my wife at home thinks you said 'so terrific,' so let's leave it there." I earned a big laugh from him and the studio audience, even though most of them had probably never heard the word before.

If you've seen a lot of old Westerns, you should recognize Smiley Burnette, another sidekick of the singing cowboys. In one movie he said to Gene Autry, "If B-R-D don't spell bird, what do it spell?"

Smiley and I were on the same bill as entertainers one Saturday afternoon in Southern California. He came up to me after my fast-draw comedy routine and complimented me on the presentation. He also invited me to his home in the San Fernando Valley so we could chat and talk shop. I enjoyed several engaging and

42

inspirational visits with Smiley—often he'd suggest a few changes in my show to make it better. He also said that sometime soon he'd help me out by making a few phone calls to just the right people to pump up my career. He admonished me, though, saying that after I became famous I should make sure to "send the elevator back down" to those struggling up the ladder of success. Before he got a chance to fulfill his promise, I read in the paper about his sudden demise. Sad. But what a fascinating talent and personality!

Smiley's son, Steve Burnette, was a gun coach/stuntman/stand-in for the movies. My stuntman friend Monty Laird brought us together for a meeting at Monty's house in the Valley. (Monty did gun stunts and bit parts in movies. Type his name into an internet search engine to read a lot about him.)

Anyhow, Steve was reputed to be one of the fastest gunslingers in movie land, so I was keenly curious to see how fast he really was. We set up my fast-draw clock in Monty's garage, and I gave Steve a holster and a Colt .45 loaded with light blanks. To make a long story short, he fired several different times, and the fastest shot was a respectable 42/100ths of a second. "Not bad for a movie guy," I thought. I immodestly explained that I thought I could get off *two* shots in the same amount of time. I set the cylinder of my gun so that it would take *two* cock-and-fires to make it fire and stop the clock. Then I thumbed and fanned a 33/100ths of a second.

Steve, of course, was amazed. I promised that I wouldn't tell anybody on the studio lots about it.

Later, Monty took me to the *Gunsmoke* set to watch Steve and the crew film a pistol-shooting scene. Someone would pull on a rope, revealing a waist-high shelf containing six whiskey bottles. Once the cover was lifted, the cowboy contestants were to draw and "hit" as many bottles as possible in a little over two seconds. Then the cover was dropped.

The stars of *Gunsmoke* weren't there that day, but L.Q. Jones, a familiar character actor, was. He got on his mark to pretend that he was drawing and shooting at the bottles. L.Q. stood there with his hand down near his gun; then they cut the action and placed Steve Burnette in the same spot. Steve was dressed the same as L.Q. and did the drawing and shooting, but you could only see his hip area during the filming. He had on the same type of rig and gun, trousers, fingernail polish, everything. He whipped out the gun and rapid-fired blanks toward the bottles—dynamite squibs burst the bottles from backstage. After the last shot, they cut the film again, showing L.Q. with a smoking gun. When they edited the film, it looked like old L.Q. had done it all. Sneaky, but effective. (I just saw L.Q. starring in *The Mark of Zorro* the other night. He is quite a talent.)

I noticed a strange phenomenon on the *Gunsmoke* set. Before the prop department handed out the guns and rigs to the make-believe cowboys, they were friendly and courteous to each other. After they strapped on their hardware, though, they took on a certain toughness and weren't nearly as polite as before. The difference was like night and day. For example, one guy tripped over the outstretched feet of another when they were both armed, and the sitting guy barked out, "Watch where you're going!"

The trippee snapped back, "Get your feet out of the way!" They didn't square off a la *High Noon*, ready to draw, but if you had set them back a hundred years, they would have slapped leather. They would have said something dripping with bravado, like, "Any time you feel lucky, make your play." Or "There's plenty of time after you go for yours." Or, in more modern language, "Don't let your 45-caliber mouth get your 22-caliber ass in trouble." Or they could have quoted Bob Hope in a western, as he stood with his hand wide open near his gun: "I ain't just dryin' my nails here, mister."

Let's not forget the lovely Joanne Dru and her husband, John Ireland (on the left), whom she met on the set of *Red River*. Joanne was the sister of Pete Leacock, better known as Peter Marshall, the famous game show host. One day, John and Joanne visited Huntington, West Virginia, near where she and her brother were born, and I interviewed them for WSAZ-TV.

Bob Denver

The late Bob Denver, if you'll remember, played the part of Maynard G. Krebs in the Dobie Gillis series. He expertly acted the part of a laid-back hippie type and brought many laughs to the audience. Later he played the lead role as Gilligan in the three-year stint of Gilligan's Island, garnering countless laughs as the innocent pawn of the several characters stranded on the island with him. Although it was short-lived as a series, Gilligan's Island was, and still is, one of the most popular reruns ever. At one point, it even outshone I Love Lucy reruns in ratings.

Bob's wife, Dreama Denver, was a native of southern West Virginia, having come from the Bluefield area many years before. When they moved from busy-busy Las Vegas, she convinced him that he would find the perfect place to settle on a hilltop above the city of Princeton, close to her birthplace. It turned out to be just that for them both.

Many years later, Bob, along with Russell Johnson (The Professor) and Dawn Wells (Mary Ann), still made personal appearances all over the country, signing books and pictures for their numerous fans. No matter where they lived, their agents organized the details and brought them together to meet the public.

One day Bob came to the WVVA-TV studios, where I worked in Bluefield, to ask for their help in making a tape he needed to send to his agent in Hollywood. After he made the tape, our general manager, Charlie Webb, thought it would be a funny bit if Bob were to show up on my weathercast. He was right.

Bob waltzed in front of the camera and my maps one day as I was explaining an approaching cold front. We shook hands, and I asked him to carry on with my weather presentation. That he did, making fun of our weather systems so comically that I ran over my allotted time by more than two minutes. What a nut! It was so funny that he appeared on the show several more times— once he even did the whole weather report by himself.

We became good friends, and I was invited to their beautiful home at the "top of the hill, end of the road." Dreama and Bob would call every four or five months, I'd visit with them over a sandwich and goodies, and we'd chew the fat about TV and movie stars we knew, along with the kooky things that happened on set. Dreama was "the hostess with the mostest" and a brilliant author in her own right—she was every bit a full partner in the goings on.

At the end of our sessions, Bob would bestow upon me three or four plastic grocery bags full of paperback books he had read. He had discovered early on that I was an avid reader of the same types of stories he liked—spy novels, Westerns, mysteries, courtroom dramas, adventure sagas, and the like. It was natural that I'd appreciate and read his books. Where before I had read fifteen or so books a year, I started reading fifty or more in the same period of time, I had so many piled up. What a bonanza! Those books were just one more reason to enjoy my visits with such interesting folks.

Bob even appeared on local *Jerry Lewis Muscular Dystrophy Telethons* with us. As an added incentive for those pledging donations, we told the TV audience that, for a hundred dollars or more in pledges, Bob would personally talk with the donor on the phone. Well, that tied him up quite a bit, but helped considerably in running us well over our quotas.

Entertainment Tonight was making a big package on Bob one time and sent their crew to our area to follow Bob around his huge home, to his favorite computer store, and other haunts. They knew of Bob's appearance on my weather segment and wanted to see him do something on it to add a little extra color to their package. I knew of a trick with a ladder, so I had Bob come by while I was pretending to weathercast, carrying one end of an aluminum ladder.

I said, "Hi, Bob. Got time to talk?"

He said, "Nope, I gotta hurry with this ladder." And off he went with his end. As the ladder moved along in front of me, I looked to the left and scratched my head, because here came Bob with the *other* end of it, too.

I said, "You look like the same guy who just went by."

"No time to chat. Gotta hurry," he said, and sailed on past again.

Then I said, "Now, how'd he do that?" as I watched his parting figure.

The trick was that, as soon as Bob went out of camera range the first time, a stagehand took the front end of the ladder, Bob ran to the tail end of the ladder, relieved the fellow holding it, and took over to come into the scene again. The strange thing was, this episode of *Entertainment Tonight* ran on our competitor's station. I wonder what they thought when they saw me doing the weather on their station. I just had to laugh.

The interesting thing about Bob Denver was that he played comedic parts so convincingly that it was tempting to think he was as inane in person as he was on the tube. Not so. He was extremely well read, as you might have already guessed, but also had a huge inborn intelligence and a naturally jovial sense of humor. I miss those visits. I miss him. Now and again I visit Dreama to bring some token of cheer, and I send her e-mail goodies and personal notes.

Along with the deep grief Dreama felt when Bob died, there was also placed on her shoulders the complexities of caring for their then-teenage son, settling the estate, and operating their commercial radio station all on her own. It takes someone super special to keep all those balls in the air at the same time, and she does it. I love her dearly and wish her the very best.

David Letterman

Everyone at the TV station in Bluefield knew about my being invited to appear on the *Letterman Show* when he was on NBC in New York City. Little did they know that it was a close call as to whether I'd be on that night or not.

Because of New York's tough gun laws, our local gun dealer, Marvin Snedegar, had to ship my Colt .45s to a gun dealer in New York City, who then brought them to me at the NBC studios. But along with this little complication, there were three of us world champions slated to go on that same evening. One was a deep-sea fisherman who had a huge fishing pole and, to make it look dramatic without a large fish on the line, had a young boy in tow to pull down on it. Dave didn't like the looks of it, so he canceled the segment. The second was a world-champion female field archer, but time got short, so the producers eliminated her.

That left the World's Overall Fast-Draw Champion to carry the load. During a commercial break they set up my table with the time clock and arranged my guns and ammo on it. Dave was acting cutesy and, as I was helping him secure the cowboy belt, holster, and gun around his waist, he said in a swishy voice, "I'd like to see something in a nice pair of Western 'boooots'." That got a big laugh, but I ignored it—smiling, of course.

I told him to grab the gun, which was loaded with small blanks, in the holster and pull the trigger. (It can't fire unless you cock it.) Then I told him to draw the gun out and smack the hammer back with his gloved left hand. This he did, and fired it into the floor. He was so smitten with the drama of it that he started firing all the other five shots at my feet. I danced around the back of the table in mock fear while he chased me.

His capers were jolly good fun and prompted more laughs, but they also shot up all the ammunition he would need later. My gun was loaded  with a very large blank for shooting out balloons, so, when I defended myself with return fire, it blasted him and his ears and visibly shocked him. He moaned, cupped his ears with both hands, and exclaimed loudly, "I'm deef, I'm deef!"

I just laughed with the audience. "That'll fix him," I thought.

I did a few more tricks. Letterman shot a 0.46-second round, reacting and drawing on the clock. Together, we managed to devour over four precious minutes of airtime. It went over well, though, according to the gang of fellow TV employees who were partying at home and awaiting my segment.

Bill Cosby

In 1993 the producers of *You Bet Your Life* thought that, as a top gunman, I might be an interesting contestant, so they flew me to Philadelphia to compete, together with a female partner, on their game show. For some unknown reason, Bill Cosby didn't get the memo

 about my being the world fast-draw champion, so he never asked about it. Aw, shucks.

We were asked a bunch of questions about movies, and we got the right answer enough times to win $1,400. Our segment played on the network a few weeks later, and Bill wound up his stint with the old Groucho Marx series just a few episodes after that. What a talent, that Cosby!

Caine Mutiny Court-Martial

Back in the 1950s, Henry Fonda and the cast of *Caine Mutiny Court-Martial* came to the stage in Huntington, West Virginia. What a privilege to see famous movie stars in person! Lloyd Nolan and John Hodiak were with Fonda; playing a minor role was an unknown young fellow by the name of James Baumgardner.

While I was working as a staff announcer on WSAZ-TV and Radio, I tried to interview Fonda for the TV audience. He said he wasn't quite ready to appear on television, but would submit to a radio interview. (At that time, the movie folks thought of TV as a dreaded competitor.) We sat down in a restaurant for the interview. I had my tape recorder on the table in front of Mr. Fonda and was asking him questions when a waitress came up and stood there expectantly. Fonda chastised her for not noticing that we were making a recording and told her to come back after we were finished. I shook hands with Hodiak and Nolan, but didn't have the chance to interview them—they had other appointments.

After the show our community theater director, Sterrett Neale, invited the cast to his house in town for after-show snacks and drinks. Among these folks was the Baumgardner fellow, who was feeling no pain when he sang in a mock hillbilly accent, "It ain't the pale moon that excites me, thrulls and delights me, or no. It's just the nurrness of yew."

Later we saw him on TV without the "Baum" or the "d" of his last name—they were calling him James Garner. Surprise, surprise.

Divorce Court

Back in the 1950s and 1960s Eddie Cochran, my Hollywood talent agent, sent me out on a lot of "cattle calls." These were big turnouts of all types of actors for parts in movies, TV shows, or commercials. The producers would ask various agents to send a certain type of person or animal over to this or that studio for tryouts. The result: great hordes of people sitting in their casting offices.

Fifty or more warm bodies could be trying out for the one or two positions needed. You had the usual "two chances" for landing a part: slim to poor, or slim to none.

I was lucky, though, and got more than my share of commercials and TV show parts. I was picked for national sponsors such as Mobilgas, Newport Cigarettes, Old Gold Cigarettes, Kellogg Corn Flakes, Phillip Morris Cigarettes, and so on. I was also chosen for parts in drama programs like *Studio One, Playhouse 90*, and *Divorce Court*. After the first run, every time one of these commercials or drama programs ran again nationally, I collected residuals. It wasn't big money, but it was better than a poke in the eye with a sharp stick.

I landed a lead role in two *Divorce Court* episodes. The thing they didn't advertise about this show was that there was no script. That's right: no script. They gave you a brief summary of that particular episode's theme, described your position and your background, and told you to take it from there. "Ad lib" was an understatement of what you were expected to do: you had to be on your toes, thinking like the character you represented and responding accordingly.

The first *Divorce Court* in which I was cast was a full hour of black-and-white footage.

The second, filmed a couple of years later, was in living color, and ran only half an hour. In both shows Voltaire Perkins played the judge. My second appearance was as an insurance agent, divorcing my wife on the grounds of infidelity. If you fell out of character—for example, if you embellished your part to make it seem as though you were president or stumbled too much—they would do the scene over.

Divorce Court never cast seasoned or well-known actors and actresses, as they didn't want anyone to recognize you across the country (it would destroy the illusion that the series was true to life). They used unknowns, Hollywood wannabes, those who'd appeared in local community theater presentations, and other actors with no national recognition. The tactic worked: these episodes were completely believable, and this particular series of *Divorce Court* ran from 1957 to 1969 in syndication. The reruns netted me some pocket change several times. One ran all across the country and on WCHS-TV in Charleston, West Virginia.

A harder-edged version of *Divorce Court* came along in 1985 and lasted another five seasons. Mind you, all this happened long before we ever heard the term "reality show."

Gene Autry

Once, in my "have-gun-will-travel" days, I was booked on the *Merv Griffin Show*, which was nationally telecast from Hollywood. On the show were the famous cowboy singers The Sons of the Pioneers, character actor Slim Pickens, singing cowboy Gene Autry, and I, in some kind of Western salute. While in the green room I had the chance to talk with Gene and Slim, and later did a few fast-gun bits on stage before old Merv interviewed me.

I was keenly interested in talking with my cowboy hero, Gene Autry, so he invited me to his office the next day at the KTLA-TV studios in Hollywood. His office was over three times larger than our living room at home. As I was shown into the spacious workplace, I noticed an old Indian squaw dummy sitting on my left near the entrance. It was weird, seeing that lifelike, stoic figure just sitting there, looking straight ahead.

When I approached Gene's mammoth desk, I noticed a beautiful pair of Colt .45s in bejeweled holsters and belt, just hanging there. Gene said that they had been a gift from Ken Maynard, a cowboy movie star hero of his own. He didn't do any fast drawing himself.

Roy Rogers and Dale Evans

Another Western cowboy hero of mine, Roy Rogers, came to our small town in the verdant hills of Appalachia. He and his wife, Dale Evans, were appearing at the State Fair of West Virginia, just a few miles away. I interviewed them for the radio station and asked him if he ever did any fast gun handling with his Colts. He said that the studio stuntmen did all the tricks and fast drawing for him, since he had no interest in furthering his expertise in that area.

He and Gene really let me down in that department, and they never seemed the same when I saw them in movies later. They should have hired me with my guns as a sidekick, so I could cover their backs.

Island of Lost Women

Sue Ladd, Alan Ladd's wife and an actress herself, decided that I'd be good for a part in a movie that Alan Ladd Productions was to make before the fiscal year ended. It didn't pretend to be a lavish production—just what they called an "exploitation film," meant to make use of their cash assets for the year's tax credit before it was too late. The title, *Island of Lost Women*, suggested something racy. Not.

The producer, Albert Cohen, asked me to come to Warner Brothers Studios to make a screen test for one of the lead parts. I memorized some lines and made the test with some studio gal who was testing, too. I don't know how great or lousy it turned out, but Mr. Cohen said that, since I had no previous experience in moviemaking, I'd just hold them up here and there on the set; it would cost them thousands of dollars on this low-budget film to delay the whole crew each time.

Yeah, sure, Al. I understand.

Okay, so I didn't get one of the leads, but I asked him to give me a bit part so I could say I'd been in a Hollywood feature film. That he did: I got a few lines near the end of the picture as the pilot of a rescue plane, coming in to save them all on the island. Big deal, but it gave me a screen credit.

The film told the story of a radio commentator and his pilot who were forced to land their plane on an uncharted island, against the wishes of the mad scientist, who had three lovely daughters. The guys meshed well with the girls, but the scientist blew up part of the island. That's where I came in. I was the pilot of the plane that came to save their sorry souls.

Ta-da! (I'm the one with his mouth open.)

Alan Napier played the part of the mad scientist. Later he became the butler Albert in the *Batman* TV series. He still looks kind of mad in this picture I found.

John Smith got the part I was trying out for and did a fine job of it—much better than I think I could have done, to be brutally frank. For a Class "C" movie, it really wasn't too bad. And getting a bit part in a Hollywood feature film is more than I'd had the year before.

Japanese To Tell the Truth

A crew from a Japanese television network heard about my winning one of my world fast-draw championships and descended on me at WSLS-TV in Roanoke, Virginia. The entourage included a soundman, cameraman, producer, and reporter/emcee. After clearing it with my boss, they asked me if I would be interested in appearing on network television in Japan.

"Sure," I told them, "Why not? I'm not on a Wanted poster anywhere." Little did I know what they called their show in Japan.

They needed three of us for their *To Tell the Truth* program, which, oddly enough, was called *Wanted* over there—it was the only English word in the opening credits. So I phoned my gun-toting friend Bill Hipes. He picked another friend of his and said they could come over to the TV station right away with their guns, loaded for bear.

Two of us had to lie about being the champion and one of us had to tell the truth. We were all dressed in Western gear and armed with Colt .45 Cowboy pistols dangling in various types of holsters. My speed rig was steel-lined and state-of-the-art in fast-draw holsters, but only shooters would notice such a detail.

The three of us were standing abreast with a half-smile on each of our faces, smirking with arched eyebrows as if we were each a big winner. We stood against a rustic background in one of Channel 10's smaller studios. I was placed in the middle and was over sixty years of age, and the other two were patently younger. They asked each of us in turn how we had managed to win the World's Overall Fast-Draw Championship.

My friend Bill, told them a phony story. He said that he had been in law enforcement, had been handling firearms for twenty of his thirty-seven years, and had a natural talent for fast-gun handling. The younger fellow on my right was about twenty-five and said that it was mostly a matter of fast reflexes—since he was still young, he naturally had the drop on older shooters when it came time to react, draw, and shoot. These two birds almost had *me* convinced.

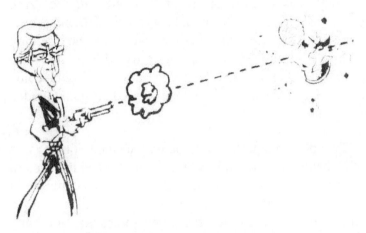

When my turn came around, I attributed my big win to extensive practice. I told the camera, "Starting a month before a contest, I increase my practice time to four hours a day, whipping the gun out and hitting targets. It's tiresome, but it usually pays off." I also said, jokingly, that the shadow of my elbow wore a hole in the wall, but that the quip didn't translate.

Our episode ran several weeks later all over Japan. They sent me a tape of the program—thankfully, it had English subtitles. Hearing my buddies and I speaking English, then being suddenly muted with a Japanese translation over top of our voices, was very strange.

Their panel was made up of five Japanese movie stars and celebrities who sat at a long table. I couldn't understand a word they said, but the translation crawl at the bottom of the screen made it clear. They also made it clear why they chose one of us as the real McCoy and passed the other two by. You can guess how many of the five votes Uncle Stanley got.

The oldest-looking of the movie stars, a guy in his fifties, was the only one who voted for me, mostly because he was suspicious. He said that it looked like a setup to him—not that he had all that much faith in my potential.

"Gee, thanks," I said aloud, watching the tape.

Then, to prove that I really was the champion, they showed me in my gunroom at home, practicing, with a bunch of my bigger trophies in the background. With any luck, that taught the panelists to have more respect for the elderly.

Lawrence Welk

Master showman and TV personality Lawrence Welk appeared at a charity benefit at a country club in Newport Beach, California in 1975. He was performing alone with his accordion and serving as the master of ceremonies.

Sylvi Lin, a beautiful world-class concert pianist, was brought to the affair by an opera-star friend who knew Mr. Welk personally. During a break in the festivities, her friend introduced Sylvi to Mr. Welk, telling him of her appearances with top symphony orchestras in Detroit, Philadelphia, Miami, Boston, Cincinnati, Stockholm, Gothenburg, Copenhagen, Oslo, and other large cities.

"Oh, then you'll perform for us today?" Welk asked, impressed.

Sylvi was taken by surprise, even though she practiced six to eight hours a day and was not unprepared for such a gracious invitation. But she had heard the tinny piano when she first entered the ballroom and had pitied the poor piano player. So she said, apologetically, "Thank you, Mr. Welk, but I need a good instrument."

"Oh, you're that good," he said.

She smiled and countered modestly, "I do need a decent instrument."

 That seemed to be the end of it. Welk resumed his duties on stage, but a few minutes later he announced over the microphone, "We have a world-renowned Swedish concert pianist in our midst today, and I'm going to ask her to play for us."

Sylvi was put on the spot, so she thought fast and played something that would help cover up the clunky piano's shortcomings: Chopin's thunderous *Revolutionary Etude*. It was received with a standing ovation. Lawrence Welk was so impressed that he put his arms around her shoulders and said, "Wow! Don't be surprised to see this lovely, talented lady on my television program."

Sylvi was surprised again when he invited her to his studio in Los Angeles the following day. There he asked her to accompany him on a ten-day tour with his musical family to the major U.S. cities as a special guest and classical artist. When they had completed the tour, Welk also arranged for Sylvi to appear on his nationally televised program.

During the tour, Welk always had Sylvi sit beside him as they traveled by plane, bus, and taxi. She discovered that he actually preferred classical music to the popular style his group offered in concert and on TV. Each afternoon he would ask her for a private performance in the auditoriums prior to that evening's show. Mr. Welk explained that, although classical was his favorite musical genre, he was a pragmatic businessman: he played popular tunes on his show to please the masses.

A few years later, Sylvi, now my wife, read in the local newspaper of Welk's upcoming concert at the Civic Center in Roanoke, Virginia. Anxious to see this wonderful showman in person once again, Sylvi and I drove from our home in White Sulphur Springs, West Virginia to the studios of WDBJ-TV in Roanoke, where I knew Welk was slated to do some promotional spots for that evening's concert.

When we arrived at the TV studios, Welk was being interviewed in the conference room. He spotted Sylvi and broke away in midsentence to give her a big hug and say hello. We were taken aback when he invited us to that evening's show and instructed his manager to arrange front-row seats for us!

Even more unexpectedly, Welk stopped the show that evening and asked Sylvi to join him on stage. She graciously accepted and made her way to the stage, where Welk introduced her to the audience as a "Swedish concert pianist" and led her to the big, black grand piano. Sylvi performed Chopin's "Fantasy Impromptu" (popularly known as "I'm Always Chasing Rainbows"). When the crowd heard the lovely, familiar melody played with such magnificent interpretative skill, they showed their appreciation with a standing ovation.

Sylvi was privileged to visit with Mr. Welk a few more times before he died in 1992. In her heart, he will always remain a true gentleman and classical music lover.

Lily Tomlin

Around 1970 or so, my fast-draw comedy act was booked for a small, low-budget nightspot called The Ice House in Pasadena, California. It was a starting place for many comedians and comics who are big names today. I'd do about twenty minutes of my routine onstage, with the people below eating, drinking, and chatting in the subdued lighting. I got some very good laughs, and so did a lot of those other blossoming comics and comedians. (The difference between a comic and a comedian? A comic says funny things, and a comedian says things funny.)

Lily Tomlin was already established as an upcoming comedienne at this point, but she used the place to polish her acts before taking them in front of supposedly more sophisticated audiences, (e.g., the ones in Vegas). She had been on the TV comedy program *Laugh-In* for some time, and the management at The Ice House was delighted to have her at bargain prices, even if she was using the crowd as guinea pigs.

Backstage, Lily was always in the company of her agent or manager, who looked like a pugilist in drag. Short and stocky, she was very solicitous of Lily and discouraged all conversation with her protégé. "Butchie" glared at me whenever I made the slightest attempt at camaraderie. I caught the hint, but it smelled a lot like insecurity or just plain jealousy to me.

I still liked comedic Lily, albeit from a greater distance. (At that time I had no reason to believe that she was anything but a red-blooded American girl.) From those days as Ernestine the Switchboard Operator to the present day, she has always been a great talent. She used to say, "Is this the person to whom I *am* speaking?" You gotta love her.

Stan Lynde and Rick O'Shay

While I was on tour in Montana with my fast-draw comedy act in 1969, I came to the town of Red Lodge, where I saw in a store some stationery with familiar cartoons on them. Drawings of Rick O'Shay, the Western cartoon character, adorned the sheets' upper left corners. I bought a couple of boxes and complimented the clerk for stocking them. He told me that the cartoonist himself lived close by. The comic strip was very popular out West between 1958 and 1977, so I made the effort to go see this talented fellow.

His name was Stan Lynde (pronounced "lined"). He invited me to see his work cabin, located just a few yards from his house, where he cranked out his comic strip every day, and showed me the various drawings that littered the desks and walls. It was a fantastic visit. He was a heck of a nice guy, too.

Stan was a punster when it came to naming his cartoon characters—the names gave you a fat clue about their occupations or personalities. Hipshot Percussion was one of his favorites. The character reminded me of Jack Palance, the movie star, whose eyes looked like two burnt holes in a sheet. Percussion was a black-hatted, mustachioed gunman, and he figured in a lot of the stories as a backup for the plucky star, Rick O'Shay, who wore the badge of a deputy marshal.

Later, just for the fun of it, I sat down and conjured up a bunch of other characters with revealing monikers to send to Stan as a joke. Here are some of my concoctions: Hiram Young, a personnel manager; Maxwell Houseman, a coffee shop counterman; Malcolm Tente and Mala Justid, both social misfits; Millie Stone, a nagging wife; Cal Ammity, an accident-prone dude; Truly Foss, an inveterate liar; Noah Borshunz, a family doctor; G. Howie Hertz, a dentist; Justin Hale, a heavy smoker; Bill Oney, a storyteller; John Quill, a florist; and Wilbur Muckenfutch, the town idiot.

Tom Clancy

From a good friend of ours, Janine Francis, who lived next to The Greenbrier Hotel in a classy community called Creekside, we got word that she had a new neighbor. Her next-door friend told her that a famous "book writer" had just bought one of the exclusive condos as a summer home. Her friend said that his name was "Tom Clouncy"—she even spelled it that way for her. I told Janine that I didn't know of any "Tom Clouncy," but I did know of a Tom *Clancy*, and I assumed that was who it was.

Since I was working as the chief weathercaster at WVVA-TV, the Beckley-Bluefield station, I sent Mr. Clancy a short note of welcome to the neighborhood, promising not to reveal his whereabouts and offering any help I could with anything he might need at the TV station. I also told him that I was the current World's Overall Fast-Draw Champion and mentioned my gun shows and my job at the station. I offered to give him a personal demonstration of my gun tricks from the shows I gave all over the globe.

Well, his housekeeping staff told him who I was. To my surprise, he took me up on my offer. He also acquiesced to an interview that our news anchor, Kevin McGraw, conducted at his Creekside residence. For lack of time, they did not list his popular books. I thought they could have at least listed the ones that had been made into movies—*The Hunt for Red October*, *Patriot Games*, and *Clear and Present Danger*, for starters. Harrison Ford played Jack Ryan in several of the flicks, which were big hits.

We made arrangements for Tom to come by my house and see my upstairs gun room; though only seven feet wide, it ran the whole width of the house. A steel silhouette target was perched at the far end along with an electronic fast-draw timer. I showed Tom some speed tricks: how I could outdraw a cocked pistol and fire multiple shots that sounded like just one long blast. For good measure, I also described how to put down a terrorist who was holding a hostage at knife point. With a mind like a steel trap, Tom was a quick study—he readily understood the intricacies of my demonstrations, so I continued.

When I concluded, he said he was interested in how I planned to take out a terrorist who was holding a hostage in front of him, not to mention why I had chosen that topic. I explained to Tom that I had seen the movie *Nighthawks* with Sylvester Stallone and been fascinated by his standoff with Rutger Hauer, the international terrorist.

In this movie they were standing on the platform beside a passenger train, Stallone pointing his automatic at Rutger Hauer, who was using a female hostage as a shield. Hauer had his head stuck well out around the hostage while holding a gun on her. He was making his demands to Detective Stallone, who was advising him to give it up as useless, but Rutger wasn't buying it. I told Tom I theorized that, if Stallone had just kept on talking with both eyes open while aiming at the same time, he could easily have plugged the guy right between the eyes. True, it would have ruined the rest of the movie, but it seemed the logical thing to do. I grew frustrated while watching the movie and said out loud, "Why don't you just shoot him, dummy? He's only ten feet away. You couldn't miss." (Apparently the characters didn't hear me, and the terrorist got away. So much for my practical reasoning.)

To demonstrate my point about handling that type of situation, I decided to let Tom do it himself. I took a black felt pen and, on a big piece of white cardboard, made a crude line drawing of a woman with a fierce-looking  terrorist's head sticking out over her shoulder and a knife at her throat.

I taped it to my silhouette target at shooting height and we stood back fifteen feet. Then I handed him my Colt Commander .45 semi-automatic pistol, which was loaded with a wax bullet propelled only by a shotgun primer—

it's not as accurate as powder and bullet, but I knew it would fly through the air at about 650 feet per second and keep a group smaller than the size of half a playing card at our fifteen-foot distance.

I asked Tom to keep both of his eyes open and, while aiming, talk nonstop, asking the guy to give it up—then, without warning, casually shoot the meanie between the eyes.

He said, "Well, how would he know that both of my eyes aren't open when I'm wearing these sunglasses?" (This was back in the days when he wore tinted glasses all the time, both indoors and out.)

I laughed. "Oh, come on, Tom. This is a hero from your novel, like John Kelly or Jack Ryan, and they don't wear sunglasses."

He cooperated, took dead aim, started talking as if he were trying to convince the guy to surrender, pulled the trigger, and hit the guy right in the forehead.

Wow! The gun would only shoot one wax bullet at a time, so I reloaded it five more times, and Tom shot out the forehead of our "terrorist." All the while, he was talking, both eyes wide open. I didn't know he could shoot *that* well. Then he told me that the basement of his home near Baltimore was a gun range where he and a few FBI friends practiced. Small wonder! (You may notice that there are bullet holes between the hostage's eyes. Tom trashed her next with similar dispatch, just to show off and teach her a lesson for involving him in such a pickle.)

Then he said about the takeout shot, "Yeah, Stan, but you could only depend on rendering such people immobile about sixty percent of the time."

I gave him a puzzled, slightly suspicious look and said, "Now, where in the heck did you get *those* figures?" He said that he'd read it somewhere. He's as clever as they come, so that was easy enough to believe.

Later, I spoke with my niece Candy's husband, Kost Elisevich, a top neurosurgeon in Detroit. He told me that a .45 slug entering a human brain at eight hundred feet per second would shut down all nerves and muscle contractions immediately for at least a few seconds. The victim would drop to the floor in a dead heap, without twitching a knife or pulling a trigger. (A couple of novels later, Tom had a woman pull that same trick on a character who was holding a gun to some other woman's head—he must have researched the possibility and found out what I had.)

By the way, which one of Tom's books do you think he himself liked the best? I always thought he would say *Red October*, but no—he chose *Without Remorse*. *That* book was a clever, interesting revenge tale, one of my very favorites.

"Why haven't the movie people gobbled it up?" I asked him.

"They're working on it," he said.

That was ten years ago. I still haven't seen it on the silver screen, but I'd love to. It's that great.

At one point, Tom opined that you can tell a man's intelligence by the look in his eyes. I smiled and said, "Is that why you wear sunglasses—so they can't tell?" He laughed. He must have been thinking of a quote from Emerson: "A man carries in his eyes the exact indication of his rank."

Clancy spent two solid hours with me in my gun room. I even offered him an arcane tidbit, telling him that a stun gun would help reduce the trauma of a rattlesnake bite. With the stun gun on, I touched my leg and zapped myself a quick one to show him that it really grabs you when that strong direct current cracks across your skin. I asked him if he'd like to try it on his own leg.

"No, thanks," he said.

Then I picked up my twelve-foot-long kangaroo bull whip. We went into the street out front so I could show him how to crack it without taking off a piece of his ear in the process. The most important trick is to jerk the whip backwards over your shoulder *very smartly*, then whip it forward fast enough to make the tip end, or the "cracker," break the sound barrier—that's the key to eliciting the loud CRACK! Tom caught on fast: within five minutes he was doing a fine job of it; he ripped out neither his hair nor an ear chunk.

I was proud to have tied up such a busy, world-renowned figure as Tom Clancy for more than two hours. I think he rather enjoyed it. I certainly did.

Willard Scott

Back in 1987 I was asked to make some weather promotions on tape with the famous weatherman, Willard Scott, of NBC's *Today Show*. He was in Roanoke, Virginia at WSLS-TV, where I was the chief weathercaster. Willard was—still is—a very funny guy, and we messed around, but we also hashed out several quick comedic bits to run several times a day on the air, promoting our weathercasts. He and I also made a short interview package to run in the news that evening.

My next brush with Willard came while I was at WVVA-TV in Bluefield, West Virginia. He had flown down from New York City in a Lear Jet and had gone to Tazewell, Virginia to make a speech (it paid $10,000, or so I heard).

The news director asked me to go there and interview Willard, my fellow weatherman, who sometimes wore his toupee and sometimes did not. I asked him bluntly what made him decide to wear his hairpiece or go bareheaded. (He called it "wearing the top up or the top down.")

Willard said, "Well, Stan, I charge $50 for appearing with the top up, and these people were too cheap to pay it, so I'm here with the top down." (Never mind the $10,000.)

Jerry Lewis

The 1960 movie production *The Bellboy* contained some voices filmed in Florida that didn't sit well with Jerry Lewis and his staff, so they sent word to talent agents that they were going to dub some covering voices over an already-filmed sequence. My agent sent me to their studios to audition for one of the parts. Only six or seven of us were trying for the parts just then.

We were ushered into the very plush private office of the Bellboy himself to find out what he needed. Jerry's office was papered with pictures of him—the place looked like class personified. He swept in with imperial majesty, decked out in a magnificent leather outfit, and proceeded to speak quite condescendingly to us. Granted, we were virtual nobodies and he was a big star, but he made us feel very unimportant and unworthy to be in his presence.

They took us each separately, placed us in front of a tape recorder, and had us read a prepared script. Jerry's people told us that we'd be notified if we got the job, and we all went our separate ways. A week later, to my surprise, I received a note saying that I hadn't been chosen, plus a check for fifty dollars for my inconvenience. That was the first time I had ever been paid for *not* getting a part. I thought it was very considerate of them.

My last contact with Jerry occurred when news anchor Cheri Haag and I traveled to Las Vegas for the conferences held prior to the airing of the first Muscular Dystrophy Telethon at WVVA-TV. They conducted instructional seminars during the day, teaching us the ins and outs of emceeing our local telethon. During each hour's time, the network presented national cut-ins that lasted twenty minutes or so; we locals took over the other forty minutes.

Jerry and Ed McMahon ran the main seminar. When it was finished, I went up to Ed and asked him to introduce me to Jerry, who was backstage, so that I could give him one of my fast-draw comedy brochures. Jerry and Sammy Davis, Jr. were well-known fast-draw enthusiasts and pretty good at handling the six-guns. I figured Jerry would be keen to meet up with the world's top gun in a sport that epitomized his gunslinger interests.

Ed obliged, explaining to Jerry that I was the current overall fast-draw world champion, and I handed Jerry my brochure. I had expected a positive reaction from what I thought was a kindred spirit.

Wrong. He took the brochure, looked at it casually, shook my hand limply, and carried on with some other business. What a shock to my delicate psyche, not receiving the recognition I thought commensurate to my elevated stature in the gun-handling world!

I smiled sickly and retired from the scene. I doubt he ever understood the full impact of that occasion.

Chapter 5: At the Maps

When I was reporting the weather on television and people who didn't know me would ask what I did for a living, I would say facetiously that I lied about the weather on TV. It usually coaxed a smile, but no one ever disagreed with the quip.

Now and again things would happen in the studio that distracted both the audience and me. Once a bulb from one of the huge Klieg floodlights blew up with a loud BANG! I guessed what it was right away, but raised my arms in mock surrender and said, "I'm not armed, Mr. Hickok."

Worse than that, one of those big lights once came loose and smashed into the cement floor of the studio while I was doing a "First Weather" segment in front of the computers. WHAM! It scared the dickens out of me. I raised my arms again and said, "Don't shoot. I'll marry your daughter. What does she look like?" Then I explained that a big lighting fixture had fallen to the floor, but luckily hadn't landed on anybody.

One time one of my suspenders popped loose in front and sprang up in the air. I quipped, "Boy, if one more pops loose, I'll be in a 'mell of a hess.'"

After one of my rotator cuff operations, I wore a sling to prevent me from moving the arm unnecessarily. Being a smart Alec, I claimed that some big guy at a restaurant had told me to shut up and I thought he said "stand up." Then I smiled and told the truth about the seven titanium screws in my shoulder.

One time an accidental close-up of my face appeared on the screen instead of a longer shot at the maps. It shocked me to see my face so magnified on the screen. It was not a flattering view, so I said, "Uh-oh, I'm no longer beautiful. I'll have to start being nice."

One morning the fog was so thick you could cut it with a knife. After issuing all the usual fog safety cautions, I told the audience that the fog was so thick the kids had been out there throwing fog balls at the cars, until one of them put a rock in one and broke a window. Some viewers believed me.

Some things you can say no more than once a year. On a wet day I once said, "Today was umbrellable, but tomorrow should be fair and cold and not much change in your pocket." Or, "It's gonna clear up cloudy and come a dry drizzle." People always wanted to know a month in advance whether we'd have a white Christmas. I'd tell them that we had a 50/50 chance of having the white stuff on the ground that day. It's still true around these parts.

Liz Forren of Fort Spring told me that there had been only one 100-percent-accurate long-term weather prediction: when God told Noah that it was going to rain for forty days and forty nights.

One night I just couldn't do anything right. The camera caught me looking the wrong way in our early weather segment. At the beginning of the main weather presentation, I forgot to turn on my microphone. Then, a minute later, I tripped on the upturned corner of the rug I was standing on, so I signaled my surrender and said, "Well, folks, I'm making a comedy tape, and this whole weathercast will be part of it."

If Halloween fell on one of my workdays, I would go "invisible"—I would wear a pea-green outfit to match the blank green chroma-key wall  behind me. The director would tweak the controls, making my clothes blend with the wall electronically and rendering everything transparent except my hands, head, and necktie. I'd be superimposed over whatever map or graphic that was showing. It looked appropriately creepy for the occasion. This picture isn't very sharp, but you get the see-through idea.

Eventually I decided that the idea had real merit. I even produced a taped package to send to the network. In it I showed a bit of tape of Melanie Walters at WCHS-TV in Charleston, when she was so obviously pregnant and doing her weather bit. "If she could make most of herself invisible," I commented, "no one would notice that she was heavy with child. Not only that, weathercasters all over the world could stand there without blocking the temperatures or weather events in any part of the map. What a boon to weather reporting!"

A rejection slip came back from NBC. Heck, they had no sense of humor; they didn't glom onto the idea the way I'd thought they would.

Forecasting in southern West Virginia is pretty tricky at times. We have all four separate and distinct seasons, and sometimes significant weather variations within a day. I explained this to my viewers on one occasion when I had goofed up the forecast. "In some other parts of the country, weather forecasting is very easy," I told them. "Take, for instance, southern California, where it's the same most of the year. What a nice, cushy job for the weather person!" Or think about Portland, Oregon, where it rains so much. I told my audience, "When you look from Portland to the east and can't see Mount Hood, it's raining. If you *can* see Mount Hood, it's *going* to rain. See how simple their forecasting is?"

It's really not fair, but our television weather maps never show the names of the states, so you have to memorize their locations and how they look in all their blankness. In the northeast you had to know the difference between Vermont and New Hampshire (a tricky thing!), so I told the viewers that Vermont was in the shape of a "V." It worked for me.

The four-corner states were another challenge to my memory, so I devised a system for calling them what they were and locating them, to boot. I called it my "U-CAN" method, making an acronym from the first letters of each state. "U" was Utah, "C" was Colorado, "A" was Arizona, and "N" was New Mexico. To drive the idea further home, I would say, "If *you can* remember 'U-CAN,' *you can* remember them all and the order they come in."

How about the five Great Lakes? The way they teach you in school is to remember the acronym "HOMES" (Huron, Ontario, Michigan, Erie, and Superior.) Not bad, but it doesn't tell you where they are relative to each other. My system not only gives you clues to their names, but also places them in their proper order. I suggested to my viewers that they think of them as "SHO-ME," with Superior, Huron, and Ontario along the top for the "SHO" part, then Michigan and Erie at the bottom for the "ME," just as they are on the map.

Let's leave the maps for a moment. While I'm talking about the TV station, let me take you to the transmitter high up on the hill above us, well over 3,000 feet above sea level. Chief Engineer Danny Via installed new equipment recently (you know—transformers, receivers, transceivers, and all things electronic and electrical). He's also responsible for its upkeep and maintenance. As you first come into the huge transmitter room, you notice a sign on the side of the first stand of equipment. You wouldn't have to speak German to translate it.

"ACHTUNG!" it reads. "Das Machine ist nicht fur Gefingerpoken und Mittengrabben. Ist easy schnappen das Springenwerk, blowenfusen, und corkenpoppen mit spitzensparken und Hellenracketmachen. Ist nicht fur gewerken by das Fumblefingeren. Das rubbernecken Sightseerern keepen das Hands in das Pockets. Relaxen und watchen das Winkenblinkenlights."

Another departure from the maps concerns a flamboyant West Virginia Secretary of State by the name of A. James Manchin. A fantastic speaker, he often dressed all in white. One day, I was interviewing him at the state fair. Everybody seemed to know him, so I was having a hard time keeping his attention—people kept coming by and he'd turn, tip his white hat, and say "howdy" to them.

As the editor of my own tapes, I was worried that so many cuts would make the piece choppy when played on the air. "They all seem to know you," I said as he shook hands with yet another fan.

"Yes," he said, "I was born and bred in these hills. Where were you born?" Without waiting for my reply, he turned again to another passerby.

Just for fun I said, "I was born out of wedlock," thinking he might smile.

He turned back to me and said, "There's some mighty pretty country up that way."

After I had just told the audience one time that afternoon storms were typical for the July climate in these parts, meteorologist Michael Haynes asked me what I thought the word "climate" meant. I told him that it was what a cat would do to a tree if a dog chased it.

For each weather report we called on our trusty weather observers to update us on their current temperatures, snowfall and rainfall amounts, overnight low readings, and floods or any other phenomena pertinent to the occasion. One evening I called Ed Pell, the manager of the West Virginia University Experimental Farm, and he answered all out of breath. I asked him why he was panting so much and he replied, "I've been out there shoveling the driveway clear from six inches of that 'light dusting' you predicted for today." But, as Willard Scott used to say, "Weather is so unpredictable, and therein lies its charm."

When one old gal answered the phone one cold night after some below-zero readings that morning, I said, "I bet your teeth were chattering when you were sleeping last night."

She snorted, "Huh. I wouldn't know about *that*. My teeth and I don't sleep together anymore."

PART TWO:
HOMETOWN HIJINKS
AND COLORFUL CHARACTERS

Chapter 1: Family

I've rubbed shoulders with a lot of Hollywood big shots in my life, but the people and events of my hometown are just as memorable—and some of them are twice as eccentric. Here's a taste of the hilarious (and sometimes bizarre) goings on in White Sulphur Springs, West Virginia.

In the Beginning

I'm glad to say I don't remember my birth, but my mother assured me that I was there that wintry day, on January 30, 1927. Back in those days, doctors paid no mind to how much a woman gained during her pregnancy, so I arrived in the comfort of my own home weighing a whopping twelve pounds. By the time she delivered, my mother, Christine Virginia Cary Sweet, who stood a petite five feet tall, was as big around as she was high. I was christened Stanley Cary Sweet, but Mother nicknamed me Sonny. Hell, everybody's mother nicknamed her son "Sonny" back then—and we have Lithuanian-born Al Jolson, star of the first-ever talking picture, *The Jazz Singer*, to thank for it. Just about the time I was born, Al came out with a song called "Sonny Boy," whose poignant lyrics turned hardcore disciplinarian mothers into sniffling softies. The words told of the depth and breadth of a mother's love:

"Climb upon my knee, Sonny Boy;

You are only three, Sonny Boy.

There's no way of knowing, there's no way of showing,

How much you mean to me, Sonny Boy."

The song's beguiling melody and tender sentiments skyrocketed the song to number one on the music charts, where it stayed for quite a while. Just plain gooey sentimentalism, if you ask me, but it seemed that every mother in the town of White Sulphur Springs, West Virginia started calling her little boy Sonny. I grew up knowing Sonny Freeman, Sonny Schleusener, Sonny Swann, Sonny Kaptis, Sonny Bickle, Sonny Jones, Sonny Casto, and probably others, but at eighty years of age, my brain cells fizzle out when I think too hard. Though family and friends knew us by our nickname, most of us Sonnys preferred to use our real names when we became adults. There were, however, many prominent men who kept the name Sonny throughout their career—Sonny Liston the prizefighter, Sonny Bono the singer, and Sonny Tufts the actor, to name a few.

I remember in particular one Sonny I grew up with, Sonny Casto, from the first grade. My teacher knew that lots of parents taught their children the alphabet even before they started their formal schooling. To get an idea of where Sonny stood academically, she asked him whether he knew his ABCs.

"Hell, no," Sonny said defensively. "I just got here!"

Service Station Stories

John Forest Cary

John Forest Cary, my mother's oldest brother, owned a full-service garage and filling station in downtown White Sulphur Springs from the 1930s through the 1950s. Uncle Forest was a big, burly man of whom someone once said he was "so ugly he was purty." He had three or four mechanics working in the garage every day, along with a couple more guys washing, waxing, and giving grease jobs and oil changes in the stalls on the other side of the building. His teenaged nephews worked and hung around the station, as well—the memories I recollect took place around the time I was fourteen and my brother Claude was thirteen. Mostly we took care of the front where the gas pumps and oil racks were, filling up cars and trucks and checking their oil and water. A lady would sing out, "Don't forget to wash the windshield—and the back one, too, if it's muddy." In those days, gasoline sold for about eighteen cents a gallon, and you gave folks full service with a smile.

"Would you please check the tires for thirty-two pounds?"

"Yes, ma'am, right away."

It was rumored that Uncle Forest was one of the town's most sought-after ladies' men. The fact that he was ugly didn't seem to slow him down one bit. To the contrary, women just seemed to take to him as if he were a big, lovable St. Bernard. When good-looking ladies drove up to the gas pumps, asking for Forest, we'd relay the message to our uncle. He would stroll out to the front and give them all the personal attention they could want; sometimes he'd even hop into their car and drive off, not to return for hours. Being the owner of his particular service station certainly had its privileges.

I remember one day three nice-looking women came by asking for my uncle. He appeared, they all took off, and that was the last we saw of him for three whole days. We later learned that these young ladies were old girlfriends from his time in New Jersey; apparently they had been partying at an old hunting cabin atop Kate's Mountain for those three days and nights. All I know for sure is that Uncle Forest returned from those three days smiling broadly and looking mighty weary. There was no doubt in my teenaged mind that Uncle Forest was a ladies' man through and through.

Being a big hit with the ladies wasn't the only thing Uncle Forest was known for around town. He loved a good fight and could be brutal. He made a name for himself as a bare-knuckled bruiser. As a lad he'd lived on a farm a few miles out of town, up a dirt thoroughfare called Tuckahoe Road. When he got bored with farm chores, he'd go up and down that dirt road in front of the homesteads, hollering at the top of his lungs for his friends Willard or Virgil or anyone else available to come out and give him a good fight.

Once he confided to me that there were two fellows in town whom he hadn't been able to best in a fistfight. Strangely enough, they weren't great big brawlers like Uncle Forest. Mr. Dillon was slim and wiry, and Del Holmes was of average height and stocky. Holmes worked for Uncle Forest at the station, washing and waxing cars. Uncle Forest said more than once that he had wrestled and fist fought each of them at great length but could not make them surrender and say "uncle." They were just too tough.

To Uncle Forest, a good fight was a good fight; it didn't matter to him who was doing the grappling. A farmer and his son came by the station one day to buy some truck parts. The son was a wiry kid about my own size and age, but he was a farm worker and as tough as they came. Uncle Forest looked at the young boy and said, "Sonny here says he can whip your ass." He was referring to me, the town boy. I was not the type to go looking for a fight.

"Oh, yeah?" says the kid.

I quickly explained that my uncle was just having a bit of fun with him.

Not really sure who was spoofing whom and not wanting to look the coward, the kid replied, "Well, anytime you feel like it, buddy."

My fun-loving uncle was trying to toughen me up, but I wasn't having any of it.

Since my brothers and I had no father figure in our lives, Uncle Forest took it upon himself to make men of us. He'd surprise us with a punch in the shoulder so hard that we'd fall backwards. Or he'd grab our hand, turn it palm up, and bend it backwards till the skin was, well, skintight. Then he'd slap our wrist.

My brother Claude would only say "ow," but when Uncle Forest smacked me on the wrist, I'd yell, "Hey, that hurts!" He called me a sissy for that and said, "I bet his nose bleeds once a month. Let's call him 'nose pad.'"

Today, some would call this child abuse, but back then, it was considered a way to "separate the men from the boys." I wonder what he'd have called me if he'd known I would later be declared "The fastest gun in the world." Would he have apologized and given me a tougher nickname? Somehow I doubt it.

Just for the fun of it and to show how strong and tough he was, Uncle Forest liked to slam his fist against the side of a car. One day, much to his dismay, he put a large dent in Claude's old Plymouth coupe. On another occasion, at my grandmother's house, his fist hit the wall so hard that it left a gaping hole in the lath and plaster. Grandma and her guests weren't impressed, so he had it repaired a week later.

To know Uncle Forest was to be suspicious of him. I remember a mean trick he once played on his handyman, Del, who asked for a few bucks' advance on his salary.

Though Del had lighter skin than most of his race, he was still considered black. Del explained that he owed the doctor money and also needed to pay a storeowner his credit balance.

"Yeah," Uncle Forest said, "you're goin' up across the tracks and see some high yeller." ("High yeller" is a racist term that refers to a person who is fair-skinned but born of mixed-race parents.)

"No, Forest," Del pleaded, "I owe some bills that gotta be paid." He left with the money in hand.

When Del's wife Bertie came by later that day asking for him, Uncle Forest, feeling devilish, told her he'd gone up across the tracks to see his high-yeller girlfriend. This news did not sit well with Bertie.

We didn't hear any more about it until the next day, when Del came to work with a bandage on his nose and a lump on his head. I asked him what had happened. He said he had only just gotten to the front porch of his house when Bertie clobbered him across the nose with a poker and, as he was falling, whacked him again across the top of the head. He had finally been able to tell her the truth and explain that Uncle Forest had intended it as a prank. She apologized, but the damage was already done. Uncle Forest always laughed at his jokes; sometimes, however, others did not find them funny. I liked Del, and I felt for him. My uncle went down a notch or two in my estimation for that thoughtless trick.

But Uncle Forest wasn't always mean. He was a soft touch for a sob story. Lots of deadbeats owed him for gasoline and services; thousands of uncollected dollars languished on my uncle's books. I offered to go visit these folks to try to collect the monies owed, but he wouldn't hear of it. Most of the people who borrowed from him, though, paid him off as soon as they got back on their feet.

We kids, on the other hand, borrowed all the time against our meager wages, and he kept a precise record of our advances. Mother had six kids with no husband to help out financially, and the meager monthly child support check that the courts exacted from my absentee father was far from adequate. We were hard pressed to get hold of the bare necessities of life, and it was not uncommon for us to go up to the garage and ask Uncle Forest for a dollar to buy hamburger, beans, potatoes, or whatever we could get for a dollar to feed several people. A dollar bill in those days could buy enough meat or other vittles to feed all of us, plus Uncle Forest, a fine evening meal that we could legitimately call supper. Uncle Forest's presence at nearly every evening meal gave us some semblance of a family life and allowed us to enjoy at least one stomach-filling meal a day.

Uncle Forest employed some colorful sayings. They're pretty crude, and they aren't all original. I'm sure lots of these sayings were handed down to him by his forefathers and friends, but I was a kid and they were new to me when he uttered them. The following are some of the most pungent and therefore the most memorable:

Of a questionable mechanic he once said, "He ain't no more a mechanic than my ass is a church."

Of a slightly built woman: "She looks like a fried fart on the way to South America."

Of a confused deliveryman: "He's like a blind dog in a meat house. He don't know which way to turn."

Of a wealthy customer: "If he had a feather up his butt and I had his money, we'd both be tickled."

To a young punk, who acted as though he could handle any man in the ring, he told him, "Why, you cocky little meathead, I'd go through you like lightning through a peach orchard."

Of a homely woman: "She's so ugly, she'd have to sneak up on the dipper to get a drink of water."

To an unattractive fellow: "I'm sure glad you're still alive. If you died, then *I* would be the ugliest man in town."

To a hard-working farmer who seldom changed his shirt: "You smell like the south end of a northbound horse."

Of a car whose engine was missing badly: "That piece of crap wouldn't pull a greasy string through a pound of soft butter."

Of a hard-headed guy who wouldn't budge: "His head is so hard, a cat couldn't scratch it."

Of a confused mechanic: "He couldn't pour piss out of a boot with the directions on the heel."

Of a sip of wine he once said, "It'll do you good and help you, too—it'll make your teeth pearly and your hair curly and childbirth a pleasure."

During the cold West Virginia winters, something was always "Cold as a well digger's ass," or chilly enough "to freeze the balls off a brass doorknocker."

"I'm going to kick your ass up around your shoulders," he'd say if we gave him any sass. Or, "I'm gonna come up there and jerk a knot in your tail."

To a stingy butcher he'd say, "That meat was sliced so thin, you could read the Lord's Prayer through it."

Answering the phone at the station was sometimes a joke, as he'd say, "Kelly's Tool Works—and so does mine."

Of a wishy-washy fellow: "He's up and down, like a commode seat."

To a gassy, smelly guy in the office: "Some animal's crawled up your ass and died."

Of the futility of someone's effort: "It's like looking up a dead horse's ass."

Naturally, he had a lot of favorite sayings about women.

When a woman went to the john, he'd say, "She went to wet her hair."

About my accidentally stumbling upon a bunch of girls at camp while they were changing their clothes, he said, "Anything you ain't seen before, just throw a rock at it."

He looked down into some buxom gal's front one day (she was showing off a lot of skin and cleavage) and said, "If you're gonna drown those pups, I'll take that one with the pink nose." She just laughed.

Of a good-looking gal who'd come in to pay for gasoline and just left, he said, "I wouldn't charge her a dime the first time."

And he wasn't kind to unattractive young girls: "She's so ugly, they'd have to tie a pork chop around her neck to get the dog to play with her."

Of a skinny girl who was collecting for a charity, he once said, "Her ass looks like two coffee beans jammed together."

Come summertime, my brother Claude and I were constantly pestering Uncle Forest to let us take his pickup truck to Blue Bend, the U.S. Forestry Service recreational area about ten miles away. Our favorite swimming hole was in Anthony's Creek, which ran through the forestry park. Uncle Forest was always cussing and fussing about our beating up his tires on that rough, unpaved dirt road, but we pleaded and promised to be careful if he'd just let us use the truck for a few hours in the afternoon.

We needed drivers' licenses, so finally, when we got a little older and had worked up enough nerve, we headed down to the State Police office to apply. The legal age for applying for a license was sixteen, but the test givers were more interested in whether you looked big enough to drive a vehicle safely than a piece of paper stating how old you were. Claude and I had learned to drive by moving cars and trucks around the garages and joyriding a vehicle up the country roads occasionally. I was fifteen and Claude was only fourteen, but somehow the cops didn't notice when we both gave our ages as sixteen and offered different months for our births. Looking back, I don't think we really fooled anybody: we showed them we could drive, and we came away with a driver's license in hand. We were two happy young fellows; no more sneaking around trying to keep out of the way of the town police. We were legal now—hot spit.

Licenses in our wallets, we set out for school to have some fun with the girls, who didn't believe we were twins and sixteen. "We're fraternal twins," we lied. "If you don't believe us, look at our driver's licenses." We told a complicated story of an early and late arrival—I being the premature son and Claude the belated. To embellish the story a bit more ornately, we'd go on to explain how Mother delivered me a couple of months early and didn't even know Claude existed until she had contractions all over again two months later. Sometimes a girl even bought it. We found perverse gratification in pulling the wool over their eyes.

When Claude passed away a couple of years ago, he still had his West Virginia driver's license stating that he was two years older than he really was.

Jerry Gallagher

If you're around a prankster, it's bound to rub off—and the mechanics-turned-pranksters in Uncle Forest's garage had learned from the best. An idle loafer or a customer standing around waiting for his car to be fixed offered a prime target for a new trick. But by far the most popular target for this crew of pranksters was a young, naïve kid who took everything at face value—in other words, me.

Jerry Gallagher, one of Uncle Forest's mechanics, once asked me to hand him a drink of water in the tin cup over by the cooler. Well, the man wanted a drink of water, so I didn't think two shakes about it. I meandered over to the cooler, picked up the tin cup that had a chain hooked to it, and filled it with water. I heard a buzzing sound, but its meaning didn't register until those electrical volts came coursing through my hand with the force of a stun gun. The cup went up and so did all the water—all over me and the garage. Fountains of laughter followed, mainly at my expense.

When I'd cooled down (literally), Jerry showed me the Model-T coil and battery they had hooked up to the tin cup's chain. As soon as I'd touched the cup, the prankster had touched the battery with a bare wire, producing enough voltage to charge the spark plugs in an old car—and jolly fun for the shockee!

As a full-service station and garage, Uncle Forest and his men worked on all types of vehicles, including the hearses from Shanklin's Funeral Home, which was housed just a few blocks from the garage. The hearse they were servicing on one particular day came complete with a corpse-laden casket in its back loading area. Jerry enlisted my help to play a trick on one of the workers, named Roger, who had a superstitious disposition and was easily spooked. I was to climb up into the rear of the hearse next to the casket and make moaning sounds when I felt the back end of the hearse being jacked up. I guess I went along with the idea because for once I wasn't the brunt of the joke.

Unsuspecting Roger was instructed to jack up the left rear wheel so the mechanics could work on the underbelly of the hearse. Earnestly protesting that he didn't want "nothin' to do with no dead people," Roger declared that he was "*not* gonna fool around with no hearse." Refusing to let Roger off the hook lest they be deprived of their fun, his fellow workers kept at it until he finally gave in. Reluctantly, he started jacking up the hearse, and about the time the vehicle started groaning from the pressure of being lifted off the garage floor, I started moaning loudly. At that same time my hand started scratching on the hearse's back window, as if something were trying to get out. Roger saw my hand and heard the moaning at the same time. His legs spread wide apart and he tore around the toolbox, knocking over a workbench as he raced outside. The rest of us laughed till our sides were splitting with pain. Later on we realized that Roger could have hurt himself or someone else as a result of his mad dash, but for the time being, we enjoyed the joke to the fullest.

Jerry told me about one Saturday when he and his buddy Tom were out in the woods drinking and squirrel hunting with .22 rifles. From their hiding spot behind an old log, they spotted a big black bear about a hundred yards away, foraging for food. Addled with just the right amount of booze, they planned some devilish fun for that old bear. Tom aimed, took the first shot, and hit his mark. Their liquor-numbed brains had given them the mistaken impression that the bear would run away once it was hit, but the old boy started charging toward them like a locomotive. Pants suddenly wet with fear, they started shooting ineffectual .22-caliber bullets at the huge beast as he galloped toward them. They loaded, shot, reloaded, and shot again, as Papa Bear headed toward them with revenge in mind. They shot at his head with both rifles, but the bullets just bounced off, leaving white bone visible and blood streaming down the his large forehead. Just as the bear was almost within swiping distance, one lucky bullet hit him square in the eye and kerplunk! The irate bruin fell to the ground right in front of their log. Whew! A close call for two drunken dumbos.

Jerry and Tom counted thirty-one tiny bullet holes peppering that poor, dead creature. Considering themselves very lucky indeed, Jerry and Tom sobered up and hightailed it home, not waiting around for Mama and Baby Bear to come checking up on Papa. I hope they learned a good lesson that day.

Uncle Ed's Service Station and Garage

Several blocks west of Uncle Forest's Gulf service station was the Amoco service station, garage, and body shop owned by Uncle Everett, or Ed, Mother's and Uncle Forest's younger brother. One would think that, in a town as small as White Sulphur Springs, two brothers competing for the same people's business would produce lots of family friction. But both Uncle Forest and Uncle Ed were just trying to make a living, and doing a pretty good job of it. They really didn't think of it as competition. It was just what they both knew how to do, and they wanted to be independent while doing it. Partnership was not their style.

Even though I hung out and helped out a lot at Uncle Forest's garage during my early teen years, I worked on a regular basis at Uncle Ed's after school during my junior and senior years. As at Uncle Forest's, I serviced the front, waiting on customers and helping out in any way I could. During this time, I came across a host of interesting characters who made an indelible impression on my young mind.

Cap Clements

Cap Clements, who worked as a mechanic for Uncle Ed, was a tall, thin fellow of about fifty. He was distinguished by his right leg, which was made mostly of wood. I don't remember his telling anyone how he'd lost it, or mentioning it much at all, for that matter, but when he got off work, he'd sit behind the counter, drinking and oiling the knee bearings on that wooden appendage.

We all knew about his ersatz leg, but our customers did not.

Cars being serviced entered and exited the garage by a large, heavy, over-the-head sliding wooden door, supported by a single coil spring on the right-hand side (the left one was broken). One evening some customers were collecting their car, and as Cap lifted the big door to let them out, it slipped from his grip.

BLAM! The door came crashing down on Cap's wooden right foot. The male customer cringed and the woman shrieked in horror as they watched that door slam down on Cap's foot. But old Cap just said, "Damn it! Another pair of shoes ruined."

These two folks watched wide-eyed as Cap raised the door again, loosened his shoe, and secured the door properly this time. They drove off quickly, obviously dumbfounded, and the rest of us just smiled.

One day I found Cap standing on the service station's restroom floor, reaching up to the ceiling to a light bulb socket without a light bulb. When Cap dared me to stick my finger in the empty socket just like he was doing, I was a wee bit suspicious. I studied the situation first, knowing I could handle the 110-volt current for a brief second or two without any great discomfort, but I wanted to be sure that was *all* the jolt I was going to get.

Upon further investigation, however, I found that Cap was standing in some spilled water on the floor—and he was balanced solely on his wooden leg. Aha! If I had touched the light socket, feet grounded in water, I would have been zapped into the next county (and maybe to kingdom come)! I refused his dare and patted myself on the back for my acute detective skills. Naturally, Cap was disappointed that I had found him out, but it didn't discourage him from trying to fool me again.

On another occasion, old Cap was in the back of the garage, working on some dents inside the frame of a car whose engine had been taken out for repair. As he was pounding on the frame with a small sledgehammer, the owner of the car walked up to see how it was coming. When Cap pounded the sledgehammer into the bent piece of auto frame the next time, he was looking up to speak with the customer and lost control of the hammer. The customer saw and heard it bounce off the frame and hit Cap full force on the shin. CLUNK! It landed hard, with a thud. Old Cap just said "Ouch," picked up the hammer, and started slamming away again. The customer stared in disbelief. I don't know whether Cap did it accidentally or just for the fun of watching people react, but he certainly got a lot of comedic mileage out of that fake leg, which, perhaps, helped ease the loss of his flesh one.

Duke, et al.

John (Duke) Traynor was a twenty-five-year-old body-and-fender man at Uncle Ed's. He was as wild as a March hare and twice as zany. One day when I asked about one of his wild stunts, he said, "I'm like a hog on ice, Sonny. I don't care whether I walk, fall, slide, or crawl."

Duke rode a big Harley-Davidson motorcycle to work and back every day from his home in Covington, Virginia, twenty miles east of White Sulphur Springs. He was astride that machine in snow, sleet, wind, rain, and ice, all on curvy U.S. Route 60, long before the days of the interstate. One morning he hit some black ice and the motorcycle flipped out from under him. He and his Hog went skidding along the dry part of the rough macadam for a hundred yards or so. When he managed to pick himself up, he had torn elbows, hands, and knees, and had worn most of the keys on his big key ring down to mere stubs from sliding on that hard pavement. He hurt for a few days, but it didn't part him from his Harley.

Old Duke and his Harley were a twosome, all right. One summer evening when someone or something had made him angry, he jumped on his motorcycle in the front of the service station, leaned it over, and cut a bunch of spinning, screaming brodies (they call them "doughnuts" nowadays). Then he popped a wheelie, lifting the front wheel up off the ground, and tore out east to Covington and home. On his way, he roared down Main Street, clocking no less than sixty miles an hour when he passed the police chief, Earl Duncan, who was chatting with a fellow on the Dry Creek Bridge.

Earl just shook his head in resignation, watching Duke tear past the fish hatchery and on out to Route 60 toward the Virginia border. The guy with the Chief blinked and said, "Well, ain't you goin' after him, Earl? He was way over the speed limit!"

Earl just commented, "It's no use. I'd never catch him before he hit the Virginia state line. It's only two miles away. He'll be back at work tomorrow, though, and I'll just slip down to Ed's and have a nice little chat with him." (He did, as a matter of fact, but it didn't do much good. Duke and his Harley had their own agenda.)

Duke had a partner-in-pranks by the name of Little (Billy) Jones, who aided and abetted him in all his shenanigans. One day a fellow from New York stopped in for gas and thought he'd have some sport with Jonesy, who he figured was just a dumb West Virginia hillbilly. Deadpan, he asked Jonesy, "How far is three miles down the road?"

To which Jonesy answered with equal sobriety, "It's the length of three fools. Just lie down and measure it."

When Jonesy met people, he'd say, "My name is Jones. I guess you know your own. I'm glad you met me."

Uncle Ed liked to brag about all the money he carried around. "Hell," Uncle Ed told Duke, "I'd feel naked if I had anything less than a hundred dollars in my pocket."

Duke loved to come back with, "If I carried more than twenty bucks on me, I'd be afraid of getting robbed." (The first liar never had a chance.)

Boasting a trim, wiry body with powerful arm muscles from doing all that auto body work, Duke was able to do a stunt I've never seen anybody else pull off. He could jump up and hang perfectly still from the long overhead pipe tire rack, which was around seven feet high, with only one hand and only one arm grasping the pipe. With just that one arm, he would muscle the rest of his body up to the bar for a chin-up. He didn't rock up and down or swing side-to-side to get momentum; he just pulled his dead weight straight up to the bar.

During the 1940s there was an internment camp just outside of town that housed German prisoners of war. The government commandeered the local airport's property and built Quonset huts and high barbed-wire fences for the POWs' incarceration. The word was that they had been captured in the North African campaign and were to be quartered nearby till the formal end of hostilities.

Strange as it might seem, some of the prisoners of the camp were allowed to be driven to and from town to work for different businesses, especially those businesses short on manpower because of the draft. The Greenbrier Hotel, which had temporarily been converted into The Ashford General Hospital for Wounded Servicemen, employed a sizable number of the POWs, and both of my uncles had three or four prisoners working in their respective garages. I remember driving Uncle Ed's workers back to camp in the evenings and how they would sing and cavort as we rolled along the mile or so back to their confinement.

The men I got to know came from all walks of life and got along with us all very well. They relished their limited freedom. As they attempted to learn English, I would try to pick up as many German words as I could by asking, "Wie sagen sie das auf Deutsch?" ("How do you say that in German?") At least, that was my crude way of saying it and learning new words and phrases.

Why didn't they try to escape? Well, never mind the language barrier—what would they escape back to? Back to the German Army, to get shot at again? They really had soft duty here, and they flat knew it.

Fritz, one of the internees, was a true-blue Nazi and didn't believe our newspaper's accounts of how the war was going overseas. Their German reports, while they had been on the front lines, had told only of their side's dramatic victories. He figured the American government was pulling the same trick on us.

Fritz knew some English already, so I explained to him as best I could that our news services were independent, calling events as they saw them, never mind whether the president liked it or not. As I'd roughly translate the headlines into German, recounting our skirmish wins in North Africa and Europe, he'd blow it off as pure propaganda—that is, until the day the papers reported our defeat in southern France. Subsequent setbacks of the Allies appeared in the headlines too, so hard-nosed Fritz finally became a believer.

Ever wonder where the letters "OK" or the word "okay" came from? Fritz told me that they came from the

105

initials of a famous countryman of his by the name of Otto Kreutzer, who did everything right. If Otto approved it, he stamped it "O.K." (I had always thought that it came from the phonetic spelling of "oll korrect," or "all correct.")

All this is by way of pointing out that Duke wasn't the only strong man around. One of the German POWs was always demonstrating feats of strength. Hermann would sit on the floor, place a handkerchief across the edge of a heavy wooden chair seat, bite the chair seat with his perfect teeth, lift it up, and stand, holding it with nothing but his teeth. Nobody else could do *that*. You could lose a lot of teeth with that trick.

For another feat of strength, Hermann would place three chairs in a row and park his head on one, his rear end on the middle one, and his heels on the third chair. Then he would remove the middle chair from the floor, stiffen his body, use his arms to rotate the chair around his midsection, then set it back under himself.

He was a virtual bridge, doing it, so I tried it and barely accomplished the feat, trembling all the while I was rotating the heavy chair. I was only five foot nine and weighed a mere one hundred and fifteen pounds, so it's a wonder I could even stay stiff enough to make the bridge, let alone muscle that chair around me. That took some strength. As a matter of fact, even at the age of eighty, I can still do forty pushups. (That's one a day for forty days.)

Beau Geste Brown

Uncle Ed's garage was different from Uncle Forest's; Ed had a cavernous work area in the far back of his much larger building. To get from the front of the station to the back of the garage was a trip within itself.

One of Uncle Ed's mechanics liked to imbibe, on the sly, swigs of Sweet Lucy, a cheap wine. He drank lots of it, and his favorite brand was Beau Geste, so the other mechanics dubbed him "Beau Geste" Brown (pronounced the Hillbilly way: "Bo-GUESS-ta"). Several times a day, Beau Geste would slip away from his workstation, traverse the width of the back of the garage, and head for another section out of sight from the other workers. This was where all the junk or wrecked cars were stored. He'd only be gone a couple of minutes, and you had to be watching carefully if you wanted to spot him taking off for the side section. Each time he'd slip away, then come right back, acting as if nothing had happened. He'd wipe his mouth off with the back of his hand and get back to work. The more often he snuck off, the more schnockered he would get as the day wore on.

One day Uncle Ed promised a customer that he would have his engine completely repaired and ready to go by the end of the workday. Beau Geste was the mechanic on this important repair, and Uncle Ed worried that his wine sipper might not finish the job by five o'clock. Not one to pick a fight, Uncle Ed wondered how he could get Beau to hold off on his sipping long enough to finish the engine repair without making him mad enough to quit on the spot.

107

I suggested to Uncle Ed that I head back to the junk section, try to find his Sweet Lucy, and then steal it. But Uncle Ed said to wait a minute while he thought the idea through. Then I told him that we'd found some red-hot pepper powder to put into the wine—*that* would put Beau Geste off his drink for the day. We could then leave the bottle right where Beau had hidden it. Uncle Ed liked that flourish on the plan, and gave me the go-ahead to find the bottle and doctor it up a bit.

I scrounged around among the old junk cars till I found his stashed bottle, which was, at this point, only half full. It was hidden under a towel in the back seat of a wrecked sedan. I unscrewed the cap and poured in some of the pepper powder. Coughing from the spicy cloud that flew into the air, I nervously put the cap back on. I gave the bottle a big shake to mix it up well and placed it back where I had found it, then peered around the corner of the big door to the area where our victim was working to make sure he wouldn't see me. When the coast was clear, I hightailed it back to the front of the station.

Those of us who were in on the prank took turns watching for Beau Geste to make his next trip to get a swig of the alcoholic hot sauce. It wasn't long before he headed toward the old cars to wet his whistle. But this time, he came out a lot more quickly than usual and made a beeline for the faucet in the far back center of the garage. When he reached the faucet, he bent down and positioned his head upside down under it to let the cold water gush into his open mouth for a solid couple of minutes. I felt a twinge of guilt, knowing how hot that doctored wine must have burned in his mouth and throat.

After the long drink of water, though, our victim went back to work and finished the engine repair on time for Uncle Ed's customer. Funny, but Beau Geste never said a word about his "hot" Sweet Lucy, and you can bet that none of us ever told him what we had plotted and done. It just goes to show that confrontation isn't always the best solution to an employer's problem.

Molly Cary:
A Woman Ahead of Her Time

Mary Ann Bland (Molly to her family) was my maternal grandmother. Most of the stories I'm poised to tell have been passed on to me by various family members, but I remember my grandma quite well. If I look into the mirror, I see her staring back at me. I am today what she looked like then. Not real flattering for a woman, but she wasn't exactly a prissy-faced doll baby.

Grandma was born in the 1880s and grew up at a Pony Express way station that her parents owned and operated in a wild, mountainous area of West Virginia. The big old log cabin was a stopping place for stagecoaches and mail riders traveling to more exotic destinations. One day a Pony Express rider by the name of John William Cary came riding through on his trusty mount and stopped long enough to fall in love with the young, blonde, blue-eyed Molly Bland. John William married Molly and carried her off to White Sulphur Springs, West Virginia, where she gave birth to her six children: John Forest,

Christine Virginia (my mother), Rives Landon, George Abner, Everette Bland, and Nellie Frances.

Grandma Molly was a strong woman. Not in the physical sense—she had little use of her left arm; as a small child, she'd fallen into the enormous fireplace at the Pony Express way station and damaged her left arm so badly that she had to favor it thereafter. I used to look at the scars and wonder what had happened. I didn't dare ask her. One didn't question Molly Cary.

Molly was strong-willed and determined. As a young woman in the days before most women even thought about having a career—or voting, for that matter—Molly aspired to be more than just a wife and mother. She had an entrepreneurial streak a mile wide. Just outside of town, on the unpaved Tuckahoe Road where she lived with her family, Molly planted a large garden packed with produce. As each vegetable came into season, she would load up the small cart and push it through the streets of White Sulphur Springs, selling her fresh vegetables to the citified townsfolk. It was laborious work, especially with only one good arm to hoe and weed the large garden, but Molly was determined to better her life and educate her children.

Every success story contains a measure of good luck. One morning as Grandma Molly was hoeing in her vegetable garden, the edge of the hoe struck something hard and solid. Thinking it was a rock, Molly dug around the solid object, only to find that it was a metal chest. Rusty and dirty from years of being buried, the chest finally creaked open, and Molly beheld the still-shiny pre-Civil War gold coins. No one in the family ever knew how many there were or the price they brought; Molly was good at keeping secrets. We do know that she quickly cashed them in at a bank in the nearby town of Ronceverte, wanting no one to know of her discovery. With the money she received for those coins, she purchased her first piece of real estate, in White Sulphur Springs on Bolt Street, and opened a small general store called the "Wee Store." Molly's good business sense and determination made her a women's libber before the term even existed.

Grandma Molly was not content to sit back and enjoy her success with the Wee Store. She soon bought other properties in town; at one point, she was accused of owning "half of White Sulphur Springs." During one land auction, Molly saw a choice one-acre lot, bid on it, and won. A half hour later, her next-door neighbor, Guy Gregory, who had had his eye on the land, arrived at the auction late and was upset because he hadn't had a chance to bid on the lot. Grandma, finding out he was interested in her newly acquired acreage, offered it to him for twice what she had paid. He accepted her offer, and Molly Cary made money without turning a finger.

Granddad John William died when I was five years old. His 1932 funeral is one of my earliest memories; I'll never forget the day the townspeople paid tribute to my beloved granddaddy. I remember standing on the sidewalk outside Grandma's Wee Store and watching what seemed like a million people (to my young eyes, at least) drive by the store to say goodbye to him—he was much loved in White Sulphur Springs. I wasn't sure what was going on, but I do remember feeling sad when Mother told me I would never see my granddaddy again. He was always swell to me, and I adored him. I just stood there on the sidewalk in stark wonderment, taking it all in to remember for a lifetime.

Granddaddy died, but Grandma lived on. She wasn't beautiful or even handsome, but her reputation and her money attracted most of the older bachelors in town. She remarried a few years after Granddaddy's death, to a Mr. Rogers. He died shortly afterwards.

Now you have to realize that by this time she was a senior citizen, and these fellows a-courtin' her were seniors as well. Death was a close companion.

Grandma married again, this time to a Mr. Atkinson. Mr. Atkinson died.

Mr. Herring was next. Mr. Herring died.

By this time Grandma was in her seventies, and we all thought, "She's too old to marry again, surely!" You would have thought that by this point any man in town would be plain scared to marry Grandma. But along came Mr. Carter, who swept her off her feet and married her amid the protests of all her children.

Mr. Carter died, too.

Ashamed as I am to admit it, when I was a teenager, just to be funny, I sent Grandma a birthday card with all five of her married names on the envelope—I mailed it to Mary Ann Bland Cary Rogers Atkinson Herring Carter.

My joke went over with her like a lead balloon. She had showed little affection for me before that dumb stunt, and she certainly offered none afterwards. Unlike Granddaddy, Grandma never showed either her kids or her grandkids any particular fondness. "I love you" wasn't part of her vocabulary. You can put the kissy, huggy type of grandmother out of your mind. Grandma was all business, all the time.

Eventually Grandma got sick and was diagnosed with TB.

My last memory is of her on her sickbed in the large master bedroom of her home on Drewry Lane, coughing and trying to put up a brave front for her children. When Grandma died, she had $320 in the bank and owned only her home. According to family gossip, a couple of her sons and a few of her grandsons had gambled and drunk most of her hard-earned money away. It seems she could never say no to paying off their gambling debts and getting them out of the messes in which they found themselves.

Christine Virginia Cary Sweet

Grandma Molly taught my mother everything she knew about love and affection. The way Molly saw it, people knew you loved them by what you did for them, not by how you squeezed and hugged and kissed them. Mother was pretty true to her unsentimental roots—but Mother's life was quite different from Grandma Molly's.

I was about nine years old when my father, Stanley Claude Sweet, decided to leave his wife (my mother) and their six children for greener pastures with another woman named Maxine. My father's decision marked my family indelibly. My siblings—from oldest to youngest Annabel Lee, Claude Iran, William Loamma, Martha, and Virginia Kay—had a hard time understanding why Daddy had left us, but Mother had even more trouble making sense of his choice. It was no easy task keeping six children fed and clothed during the Depression. Many days Mother thought she would have to split us up in order to keep us alive, but somehow, with her brothers' and mother's help, she managed to hold us all together. Mother, bless her soul, was our mainstay. I think bitterness steeled her, made her determined to show Stanley she could get along without him.

Before Mother died, my father made a trip back to West Virginia. He'd moved to Florida early on in the divorce, probably so he wouldn't have to pay child support, but apparently he wanted to visit his children and ask my mother to forgive him for what he had done to her. Father knocked on my mother's door (she was living in the house where Grandma Cary had died), and when Mother opened the door and saw a very old Stanley Sweet standing on the porch, she said calmly to him, "I buried you fifty years ago, Stanley—now go away!" and promptly shut the door. Mother wasn't one either to forgive or forget.

Mother had her own way of teaching us kids right and wrong. "You'll be clean when you leave this house for school, because anyone can afford a nickel bar of soap," she would say, or "Blue and green aren't fit to be seen." Or "Fools' names, like their faces, are always seen in public places."

"Don't say 'ain't,' because 'ain't' ain't right," she would admonish. "Don't say you're 'through eating.' You go 'through the door' and you're 'finished eating,'" was yet another one. Speaking good English was important to Mother; she knew it would help us succeed, so she kept up the grammar lessons: "Say 'may I' instead of 'can I' when you ask permission. 'Can' implies you might not be able to do it."

Mother had one particularly strange knack: any time she wanted, she could stand in the middle of a lawn flowing with wild clover, reach down, and pick out a four-leaf clover. Mother could always find the extra fillip that nature tried to hide. Meanwhile, I could look for hours and never find a single four-leaf clover. The only

115

clue she would give me was "Look for four leaves, not three." Didn't make much sense to me then—and it doesn't now, either. Mother used to save those four-leaf clovers, figuring it couldn't hurt since they bring good luck. Most of her books contained at least one four-leaf clover flattened between the pages. Another of Mother's peculiarities: she never experienced a menstrual flow.

Mother lived to the ripe old age of eighty-eight, probably because she never inhaled when she smoked her ever-present Camel cigarettes. She always had a cigarette in her hand or on the ashtray, but like Bette Davis she just puffed and blew the smoke away without drawing it into her lungs. I still miss and love her, though she's been gone since 1993. Her lessons live on in me and my children.

Chapter 2: Town Folk

Old Doc Myle

W. E. Myles, M.D. meandered in and out of my life
 during my childhood and young
adult years. A crusty but much-
loved old devil, Doc Myles was
White Sulphur Spring's resident
general practitioner. He had
delivered half the babies in
town, most of them in their own
homes.

One day a well-known local
high school football star came into his office with a
problem concerning "a buddy of his." It seems that said
"buddy" had visited some ladies of the evening in the
Charleston, West Virginia red-light district known as
Frye's Alley. This "buddy" was concerned that he might
have picked up some kind of social disease. After
describing to Doc Myles some of the symptoms his
"buddy" was having, including burning urination and
unwelcome drainage "down there," he mentioned that his
"buddy" was just too embarrassed to come see the doctor
in person. He was, as a good friend, checking into it for
him.

Doc, being a wise old bird, slid his glasses down his
nose, looked him squarely in the eyes, and said, "Why
don't you just pull your 'buddy' out and let's take a look
at him?"

One of my own experiences with Doc Myles was less traumatic, but pretty important to me nonetheless. In January of 1950 I was coming down to my last quarter of schooling at The Ohio State University. Up till then the government had covered all my college tuition because of the time I had spent in the U.S. Army Air Corps, but I discovered to my dismay that I didn't have enough credits left on the G.I. Bill to pay for the rest of my tuition. In order to finish that last quarter of school I needed a few hundred dollars. I was so close to getting my degree—but heck, who had that kind of money in those days?

Desperate, I took my mother's advice and went to see Doc Myles to ask him if he would co-sign a promissory note from our local bank. After I had explained my situation, Doc said, "No problem, son," and signed the note. What a relief—now the bank would lend me enough money to pay my tuition, since Doc had guaranteed the bank that he would repay the loan if I didn't.

On my way out of his office, I thanked Doc Myles profusely and promised that I would pay off the loan as soon as I finished college and got a job. Just as I was about to cross the threshold of his office door, Doc said to my back, "By the way, son, who in the hell *are* you?"

Mother laughed when I told her the story, but understanding what it all meant brought tears to her eyes.

Thanks to Doc Myles, I went on to finish that final quarter at O.S.U. and got my degree in business administration. Then, true to my word, I paid the bank back with the money I earned on my first job—as a collection manager for The Michigan Bank in Detroit.

Renzie Ryder

Renzie Ryder was a wiry old codger who lived on a one-lane road up in the country between two small hills. We were neighbors: I owned an old farmhouse and thirty acres, most of them hillside, snug up against the curves of his homestead and across from a golf course. Renzie would come by once in a while to say "howdy" and wisecrack about something or other as I was working.

Some young fellow roared by in a beat-up old jalopy on the tiny road out front one day. Renzie remarked dryly, "He ain't goin' nowhere, but he's gotta git there right now."

On the second floor of my old farmhouse, along the baseboard of my bedroom, I had just installed a new electric heater that warmed the liquid inside it, supposedly to help maintain the room's temperature after the heater shut off. I was complaining one day to Renzie that it never got hot enough to do much to heat the room—it was so lukewarm you could lay your hand smack-dab on top of it while it was on and never get burned.

Renzie said, "Stan, you need to take that old horse blanket there and throw it over that heater. No use both of you freezin'."

Renzie always had a lip full of snuff, and the brown juice from it trickled down along the right side of his mouth and dried there. I always thought how disgusting it must be when he kissed his wife Myrtle. Then one day I saw Myrtle—she had a puffed-out lower lip and a line of brown spittle down the *left* side of *her* mouth.

One night, while I was sleeping upstairs in the bedroom, I heard some thumping around in the shed outside the window below. I thought it might be either a large animal rummaging around for food or a thief, so I took my .45 Colt semi-automatic pistol and flashlight and leaned out the window. The powerful beam of the camp light cut through the darkness, and I spied old Renzie at the door of the shed. He yelled up, "It's only me, old Renzie. I'm lookin' for that crowbar I forgot and left with you today."

He was so colorful a personality that I had him on my disc jockey program on WSLW Radio from time to time, just to see what he'd come up with. He certainly added country humor to my record interruptions, but one day he broke us all up. We were talking about all his animals on the farm and how well his garden grew, and I mentioned that with all the cows and horses he had, he'd never be short on manure for fertilizer.

His comment? "Don't need to buy no fertilizer with that cow shit all over the place." The management wouldn't let me interview him anymore after that.

The preacher came to see Renzie one day and was admiring his crop of corn, tomatoes, and cabbage, which were ripening nicely in the late morning sun. He said to Renzie, "That's some beautiful, fine work that you and the Lord have done to this place."

"Yes," said Renzie, "but you shoulda seen it when the Lord had it by hisself."

All his friends say that he was the originator of that now-famous comeback.

Here's another one that several old-timers attributed to Renzie, but it sure smacks of a joke. In 1933, a farmer from up Route 92 about ten miles had a tough old mother-in-law who was kicked in the head by his feisty mule and died from a concussion.

A long line of pickup trucks, horses, and buggies gathered around the funeral home when the old gal was about to be put to rest. Marshall Shanklin, the funeral director, edged over to Renzie, who was decked out in new overalls, and said, "I thought this old biddy was a tough, mean broad, but I see she had a lot of friends who must have thought pretty much of her."

Renzie said, "Marshall, they ain't here for the funeral. They come to see if they can buy that mule."

Hog Bill Alderman

You might think that "Hog Bill" Alderman got his nickname because he raised hogs. He certainly did look as though he slept in a sty. The story was, though, that he worked for a lumber company, cleaning out the muddy ruts the log-laden wagons made, so that he always looked filthy. He was stooped over and carried a broken-down double-barreled shotgun over his shoulder, along with a bag of cabbage to sell.

Hog Bill would say, "You wanna buy some cabbage, some fine cabbage? I growed it myself. I growed it myself." He tended to repeat everything, and he was very hard of hearing. Countless stories circulated, most of them conflicting with each other, about his life up in the hills along the Virginia state line. Some said that he lived in a cave and had a big garden and a whole bunch of pigs. The article cited below, however, makes no mention of swine.

Dana Ford Thomas of the *Covington Virginian* newspaper visited old Bill at his hut in July of 1954. Since he had sworn to shoot trespassers on sight, Thomas enlisted the help of Bill's friend, Ervine, who would visit the old hermit to bring him food and clothing and plugs of chewing tobacco. Not knowing our town's name for him, Thomas called him "Wild Bill," but not to his face. In the end, Ervine's ambassadorial presence did the trick: Bill allowed Thomas to snap his picture and take some shots of his abode.

The old man's hovel was high atop Allegheny Mountain. True enough, he had lived in a small cave until Ervine recruited some buddies to help build him a wooden tarpaper-covered shack. It wasn't much bigger than a backyard shed, but it kept him out of the elements. Inside, it looked like a trash bomb had gone off, but Bill had a wood cooking stove, a big water pot, and a place to sleep.

Hog Bill was leery of strangers and the law. He said to Thomas, "I been clubbed nigh to death. Been cut up bad. Cut up bad. But I ain't broke down. Broke down. 'Tis so. 'Tis so." Then he started telling about a bear that had trespassed on his domain. "Set a bear trap oncet, I did. Woke up in the middle of the night. Heard a bear a-hollerin' and a-hollerin.' 'Tis so. 'Tis so. Took my shotgun to the trap, close as eight foot. Close as eight foot. Bear big as me. Big as me. Bear's front paw caught in the trap. In the trap. Runnin' 'round and 'round a tree. I leveled my shotgun, I did. Damn thing misfired. Misfired. First time it ever happened. Damn thing no good. No good. Throwed the damn gun down. No good. Took my knife, started to cut that bear's throat. Bear skeered, he was. Jerked 'way from the trap. Left his paw in the trap, he did. 'Tis so. 'Tis so. Wouldn't stay an' fight. Ran up the mountain. Couldn't ketch 'im. Couldn't ketch 'im."

At the logging camp Hog Bill used to pick a fight with whoever was known as the strongest man there, just to show how tough he was. He wasn't all that large a man, and they say that one time he was beaten so badly he almost didn't recover. That episode and the other beatings he took were probably responsible for his mental condition.

No one seemed to know what secret kept the old man up on that mountaintop. He apparently lived in mortal fear that someday the wrong people would appear, maybe to take him away from his Spartan homestead. When he did brave the elements and the possibility of capture to come to White Sulphur Springs, he'd trade cabbage or corn for shotgun shells, beef tallow, and bones for making soup.

He bought a plug of tobacco one day from Perry's Store, and Milton Perry was counting his change for it. Hog Bill kept his coins rolled up in a tattletale-gray handkerchief, so Milton drew out what he needed and said, "That'll be sufficient."

Hog Bill replied, "You been a-fishin'?"

"No, no," Milton said, a little louder. "I said, 'That'll be plenty.'"

To which Bill said, "Oh, you caught twenty?"

"Poor soul," said Milton, with compassion.

Then old Bill said, "Oh, you broke your pole? Too bad, too bad."

Now, that's what Milton *said* he said—mostly, I think, just to be funny, figuring that we would all believe it, since it was so like Hog Bill.

The Burning Cross

It was around 1944, I'd say, when I was seventeen years old, that an article came out in the newspaper about

124

 some Ku Klux Klan (KKK) members in Alabama who had set a large wooden cross afire on top of a hill to warn folks of their fury. The KKK devoutly believed that black folks were "unrighteous" when they availed themselves of life, liberty, and the pursuit of happiness here in the U.S.A.

In general, the people of White Sulphur Springs recognized that everyone, regardless of race, was entitled to the God-given right to speak and act like a regular citizen. Most of our local folks paid little attention to the article, except to feel thankful that we didn't have to worry about such things in our little hill community. Those things happened to other people in other cities, not to us.

One night shortly afterwards, though, a huge, flaming cross appeared from the darkness, lighting up the whole south side of Cemetery Hill. The town folks didn't know what to make of it, finding it hard to believe that a nest of hooded Klansmen was working its threats in our town.

That burning cross sure did rattle the townspeople, especially our black citizens. How dare the KKK bust in here and commit such a terrible act? It gave our quiet town a bad name and smacked of terrorism.

A few weeks passed and nothing else happened, thank goodness. The town police, the State Police, and the FBI investigated for over a year, but never found the culprits or evidence of any links to the KKK. Life went on as usual.

But just a few years ago, out of the blue, I received an e-mail from an old childhood friend relating the following confession:

"There were several of us, ranging in ages from fifteen to eighteen, sitting in O'Farrell's Restaurant in the middle of downtown White Sulphur Springs. We were just shooting the bull, talking about the state football and basketball scores, who looked the best, who looked the worst. Then, of course, we talked about girls or women—on that we could go on forever.

"Someone mentioned dynamite. How you had to cover it up to make it blow inwards. We talked about everything and somehow someone mentioned burning a cross. We had all seen pictures of burning crosses in the newspaper or heard about them on the radio, but no one among us had ever actually burned a cross. No, we didn't have anything against our own colored people. It was just a fun prank we wanted to pull, without thinking of the consequences.

"One of the guys, who name was Junior, suggested that we should find someplace in town to burn a cross for ourselves. Why not? One guy said he had two two-by-fours. One was six feet long and the other was twelve feet long, just the right size for a large cross. Another guy said he had access to Collins' Service Station, where there was plenty of used oil and even some gas in cans.

Another fellow piped up and said he knew a place where he could get some old inner tubes to help with the burning, and another kid said he had a shovel and plenty of nails.

"By this time we had just about everything we needed to burn our own cross. We jumped into action, but three hours passed before we could get all our stuff together and into the back of Junior's pickup truck.

"We still had some planning to do. Where do you burn a cross? Of course, Cemetery Hill, one of the highest places in town, was our answer. We wanted everyone in town to see our cross burn. How would we make our getaway? Who would actually light the cross? Minor details, but we weren't going to leave anything undone; we would plan this act down to the smallest detail. Or so we thought.

"All the supplies that were needed would be taken up to Cemetery Hill in Junior's pickup, along with several of the guys. Once the cross was up and ready, two of us would stay behind and light the cross, then hightail it out of there in the truck. The rest who'd helped erect the cross would leave before it was lit and then cut through the grounds of The Greenbrier Hotel, walk through the golf course, and meet at the local airport a couple of miles away. The rest of the gang would be at the airport, ready to pick us up.

"Once the cross was lit, we had to run like the wind to get out of the area so we wouldn't be caught. One thing we hadn't planned on was running in the darkness at three o'clock in the morning. We thought we heard dogs, and then we were sure we heard dogs. We ran harder, only to fall harder. Each time we fell, another part of our bodies hurt. And all the time there was this huge fire on the hill behind us, burning brightly for all the world to see. We were scared to death! Finally, we made it to the airport and joined the rest of the gang and shuffled on home. What a sorry and sad bunch we were. Where was the fun in our accomplishment?

"We didn't know it at the time, but a guy by the name of Bill Rabe happened to see the fire on the side of that hill and immediately called the local fire department. When the emergency siren went off, it was so loud it woke just about everyone in our little town. People all over got up and watched the firemen having precious little success putting out an oil and gas fire.

"The town police, the West Virginia State Police, and the F.B.I. were there the next day, looking at what was left of our burning cross. Even though the town was abuzz, no one in the poolrooms, barbershop, stores, service stations, diners, or Dairy Queen knew a single thing about that burning cross. No one could even venture a guess. Although the investigation went on for about a year, not a word was murmured about who was responsible for burning that cross.

"I never knew the names of all the other fellows in our group of arsonists. We never talked to each other about the incident, and we still don't talk about it today. There had to be at least ten of us, and we scared a town like it had never been scared before. Yes, we were ten of the stupidest young guys in the world. Oh, the things you never want your children or grandchildren to do!"

My childhood friend and his fellow firebug Junior have since passed away, and the others who were involved never came forward. But if by chance any of them should read this story, I'm sure they'll smile and quietly thank God that no one was hurt and they were never caught.

Young Caddies

The fabulous White Sulphur Springs resort known as The Greenbrier Hotel and Cottages covers over 1,200 acres and employs over 1,200 men and women in the peak seasons of spring, summer, and fall. It was and is by far the biggest employer in the region. Back in the day, though, the resort still occasionally wanted for manpower when the hotel was full to capacity. The staffing shortage hurt keenly at the golf courses, where they often lacked for caddies.

Golf carts were not as prevalent in the 1940s as they are now, so the caddies had to haul the heavy bags of clubs over their shoulders by the straps. Needless to say, after eighteen holes of golf—sometimes even thirty-six—that kind of toting became a pain that a pill couldn't reach. Those who were slight of build had a very rough time of it. Even larger men were exhausted by the end of a Greenbrier golfing day. They slept on their own side of the bed those nights.

The hotel management used to call our high school to enlist caddying volunteers from the junior and senior classes, even though it meant that the boys would lose class time to fulfill the job. Since The Greenbrier offered such a boost to the local economy, the principal would allow the boys to cut class to accommodate the resort.

You had to be sixteen years of age to qualify, and I was just barely of age the first year I caddied. My brother Claude was only fifteen, but he passed himself off as me when I couldn't make it. He was just as big as I was, we both had butch haircuts, and we "looked so much apart, you couldn't tell us alike."

The tall, thin, wiry old caddy master, Pop Clements, got suspicious one day and played a trick on Claude. My brother was masquerading as me and was caught off-guard when Pop asked him, "Is that you or your brother?"

Without thinking, Claude answered, "My brother—I mean, I mean…"

Pop and the other caddies laughed, but they let him caddy anyhow.

Claude had a very wry wit and a buttoned-down humor he'd pull on you once in a while. When I went to visit him in Detroit, we went to one of his favorite restaurants for lunch. An older, saucy waitress came up, pad in hand, to take our orders.

Claude really surprised me when he said, "Wash your ass with the hamburger?"

She was startled. "What did you say?"

130

"What you ask for the hamburgers?" he answered.

"Oh, a dollar ninety-five," she said.

Then Claude said, "Finger in your ass too much?"

"What did you just say?" she demanded.

He replied innocently, "Don't you figure you're asking too much?"

"No," she said. "It's as good a price as anybody else's."

I was cringing with mortal fear that she'd hit us both over the head with a plate or something.

PART THREE:
SEEING THE WORLD

Chapter 1: U.S. Army Air Corps—North Africa

When I graduated from high school in May of 1944, World War II was at its peak—D-Day landings, U.S. troops liberating Cherbourg, the Allied invasion of southern France. It was only a matter of time before I would be drafted into the regular army as a foot soldier. That outlook held no appeal for me: I imagined myself as an ace fighter pilot in the big blue sky for Uncle Sam.

At seventeen I was allowed to sign up as an air cadet in the U.S. Army Air Corps, subject to indoctrination on my eighteenth birthday. But by the time I was called up in 1945, well after my eighteenth birthday, the war in Europe was winding down and the Air Corps had way too many pilot trainees. The Air Corps was also flooded with bombardiers and navigator trainees. My dream of being an ace fighter pilot never got off the ground.

I had other options, though. The Corps thought I would do well in Military Intelligence, but I knew I would never learn anything about airplanes in that branch of the service. The next best thing to flying an airplane was working on them. So, off I went to Keesler Field Air Force Base in Biloxi, Mississippi for training as an aircraft mechanic.

What a greenhorn I was about military life—not to mention my lack of knowledge about airplanes! But after only six months of basic training and classes on bomber maintenance, the Corps sent me to Port Lyautey in French Morocco (it's now called Kenitra, Morocco) in northwest Africa. A young, naïve hillbilly met another world.

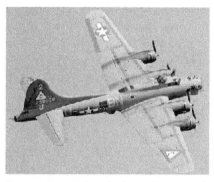

My squadron was part of the 9th Air Force, and I was assigned to a B-17 Flying Fortress heavy bomber for maintenance duty. "Last year I couldn't even spell 'flying fortress mechanic,' and now I are one," I thought to myself.

The B-17 Flying Fortress served in every World War II combat zone, but it was best known for its daylight strategic bombing of German industrial targets. Some of the B-17 models were equipped with lifeboats for sea rescues, but the planes were primarily used for these daylight raids. The most famous of the B-17 bombers was called the Memphis Belle—it completed over twenty-five bombing missions in European territory. I also worked on the B-24s, the ones they jokingly called the "B-dash-2-crash-4s." Apparently, their record of service wasn't worth bragging about.

Crew Chief was my Military Occupational Specialty (M.O.S.), a position affectionately known as a "ground pounder." I was fortunate enough to get the rank of crew chief because of my "extensive" training as a mechanic on bombers. Don't laugh: my few months of schooling on bombers far exceeded the training my assigned maintenance crew had encountered. Some of my crew were sergeants—I'll admit it was a little strange for a private first class to be ordering these superiors around. But everyone cooperated; after all, we had quite a job to do, tearing down faulty engines and replacing all the offending parts. We made them all new again. Yeah, sure.

Technically, I was a crew chief, but now and again, when we were shorthanded, I flew as a flight engineer. I knew more about the inner workings of the B-17 than the pilots, but had never actually flown a B-17. The pilots knew it and rubbed my nose in it every chance they got. My first time up as a "fly boy" was certainly one to remember.

Satellites didn't exist back then, so the task of photographing the entire earth was done manually by flying 20,000 feet or higher over the earth. These missions of photographing sectored-off land masses into grids and overlapping each picture by a few miles were referred to as the "Casey-Jones Missions." They were peaceful enough, but still a tremendous undertaking considering the instruments available to us back then. It was on one of these missions that I took my first flight up into the wild blue yonder.

About an hour or two into the air, I told the copilot I "had to see a man about a dog."

"Go back into the bomb bay and find the funnel that's hanging on the superstructure. Use that," he said.

We were flying about 260 miles per hour, pretty fast for that day and age. The catwalk back to the bomb bay was about a foot and a half wide, so I had to hang on tight to the hangers to get to the spot where the funnel hung along an upright beam. I grabbed the funnel, which was

hooked to a long length of plastic tubing. The makeshift pit stop works quite simply: the funnel releases its contents through the plastic tubing, which leaks to the trailing edge of the left wing. The slipstream vacuum draws out the contents, spraying it out into the whipping wind behind the plane.

This plan would have worked just fine, except that when I started relieving my bladder, the copilot flicked a switch and opened the bomb bay doors ever so slightly. You don't have to be a genius to figure out what happened next: air rushed into the confines of the empty bomb bay, whooshing and swirling the urine all over the place and misting a fine sprinkle all over me. New-guy initiation.

It didn't stop there. On the way back to the base, the pilots decided to give the new guy an "up close and personal" look at the countryside below. At times we were flying so low we were below the tops of the trees. I found a comfortable spot in the nose of the airplane where the "bombigator" (bombardier-navigator) usually flew and just closed my eyes and prayed.

We flew just a few feet above some poor Arab shepherds, who scattered hither and yon when they heard and saw the bomber approaching. We blew over their tents, and animals tore off and ran every which way, knocking down anything and everything that got in their path. It was a dirty trick to play, and I'm sure those shepherds applied some less-than-flattering epithets to us crazy Americans.

As we were about to land back at the base, the pilot handed me a large crank and told me to "see to it."

"See to what?" I asked him. "What do I do with this?"

Laughing, he told me where to stick it.

After that humorous exchange, the pilot explained that I had to go into the bomb bay against the forward bulkhead and crank down the landing gears, then lock them securely in case they didn't come all the way down by hydraulic power. I "saw to it," and we continued home. So much for my first time in the air.

On another of my expeditions as a flight engineer, we flew over a huge area of solid rock situated at the crossroads of the Atlantic Ocean and the Mediterranean Sea. "That's the Rock of Gibraltar," someone mentioned, "the most famous rock in the whole world."

Wow! How many times had I heard my mother or someone use the image of that famous rock? "He's the Rock of Gibraltar," or "I'll do that when the Rock of Gibraltar crumbles." It really did exist—and here I was, flying over it and seeing it at an angle that most folks don't get to enjoy. I spied a huge flat area at the bottom of the rock. Since the town of Gibraltar had no access to fresh water at the time, the residents used this area to catch rainwater.

This spectacular rock monolith covers a land area of about six square kilometers, or four and a half miles. The Rock of Gibraltar has stood guard over the Mediterranean for centuries, making it the focus of a continuous struggle for power. In ancient times, Gibraltar marked the limit of the known world. For sailors, passing the Rock of Gibraltar meant swirling to certain destruction in the bottomless waters at the end of the world. I wonder what those sailors of old would think if they could have seen what I saw that day?

Dakar, the capital city of Senegal, located a few miles from Port Lyautey on the Cape Verde Peninsula on the country's Atlantic coast, was a popular destination for soldiers on leave. It was also an ideal place to shop for the folks back home, because you could find and buy anything you wanted there. That's where Luke the Spook, a skinny, hairy little varmint of a monkey, came from. Luke was just an average monkey who'd been brought back to the base after an alcohol-lubricated shopping excursion and then turned loose. Once his owner sobered up, maybe he hoped Luke would run off, but Luke quickly became the squadron's mascot and our littlest soldier. Most of the soldiers developed a habit of putting candy in their front pockets just to see Luke reach in and drag it out to eat. Luke was known to grab more than candy at times.

I doubt that Luke weighed more than thirty pounds, but one day he was up on the very tip of the right wing of my B-17 charge, screeching and jumping up and down. Lord only knows what was bothering him, but using maximum leverage he was rocking that entire megaton flying machine. Maybe someone took his candy.

Not everyone in the squadron was emotionally attached to Luke. Being an inquisitive soldier, Luke got into our Quonset hut one day and made the mistake of digging into the personal belongings of a salty little tech sergeant. We all laughed pretty hard as Luke tore the sergeant's belongings asunder. When the wiry non-com came in, drunk as a skunk, and discovered that Luke had wreaked havoc with his personal property, he grabbed Luke by the tail, dragged him off screaming his lungs out, and slung him into the tall weeds outside. My bunkmate Gerald Joubert and I just stood there, watching our cute little fuzzy-faced feller getting his just deserts. We complained, but we were outranked.

Animals sense danger we humans can't understand. Luke used to walk with his tail up in the air under an engine with the propeller spinning. Those propellers spun fast enough to rip off his tail, even at idling speed—and they rotate so close to the ground that there are only a couple of feet to spare. One day I watched Luke walking on all fours toward a spinning B-17 propeller with his tail sticking straight up in the air—bloodshed was just a tail's length away. Strangely, though, just as he reached the spinning propeller, he lowered his tail and walked under it without even trimming a hair. His tail stood erect again on the other side of the propeller. Go figure.

But even Luke didn't sense the danger he was in one day when, unbeknownst to us, he climbed up into the wheel well of the bomber aircraft we had been working on. (The wheel well is the space into which the landing gear retracts after takeoff.) The plane was scheduled for a post-repair test run. It began to taxi to the end of the runway for takeoff.

I drove the Jeep to the opposite end of the airstrip to inspect the aircraft for oil leaks as it left the ground. Just as the plane soared directly over me, I saw a long, furry tail sticking out around the edge of the wheel well. If the pilot retracted the landing gear, it would be the end of Luke. He would be crushed, and the hydraulic lines that raised and lowered the wheel would be smashed.

Right away I raised the pilot on the radio and yelled, "DON'T RETRACT THE GEARS!" Panic-stricken, I saw the gears starting to rise.

"DON'T RAISE THE LANDING GEARS!" I yelled again.

I heard the pilot curse over the radio and saw the landing gears stop in midair. Very slowly, the huge aircraft turned around and made an impromptu landing.

Once the bomber had landed, several worried soldiers gathered around to see if Luke had come through in one piece. We all stood by the huge wheel and peered anxiously up into the well. There was Luke, clinging to the hydraulic lines with all the strength his little arms could muster. His eyes as big as teacups, Luke fought and screeched like a banshee to stay attached to the tangle of mechanical devices he had been clinging to for safety. We had one heck of a time pulling him loose. Luke never again searched for treasure in the wheel well.

I can't remember what eventually happened to that dopey monkey. One day he was with us, and the next he had gone in search of sweeter pockets.

It's an awesome sight, a long row of B-17 Flying Fortress bombers lined up with their noses all facing the taxiway, poised to take off at a moment's notice. Pilots and crew alike loved those planes. But all that beauty comes at a price: even though there were no war emergencies to plague us then, working around bombers was a dangerous occupation. One incident I'll never forget occurred when one of my fellow crew chiefs, Gary, made the fatal mistake of trying to protect his precious machine.

It happened so quickly. An oxygen truck rolled into Gary's bay, slowly, at about five miles per hour. The chubby guy who drove the oxygen truck braked as he approached the bomber, but found to his dismay that the brakes didn't work. Instead of steering the vehicle hard right to miss the plane, he panicked and bailed out of the truck, hitting the ground running hard. With no one steering the oxygen truck, it headed directly for the Number Two engine

propeller, where Gary was standing. Gary saw the dilemma and rushed forward to try to stop the oxygen truck from hitting "his" aircraft. But the momentum of the heavy truck was too powerful and it pushed him backwards, ramming his head into the down blade of the propeller. Gary was killed instantly as the whole aircraft shuddered in response to the hit.

It was a sad and horrifying experience for my squadron. After that incident, I never again took my safety for granted.

I only spent nine months taking care of those B-17 bombers, but it was a nine months I'll never forget. Learning the military way of life and encountering a foreign country's culture initiated a young West Virginia hillbilly rapidly into the real world of the 1940s and '50s.

Chapter 2: Getting Started in Television

By 1949 I'd finished my tour of duty in the Army. I spent a couple of years attending Marshall College in Huntington, West Virginia and then went on for one term at Case Western Reserve University in Cleveland, Ohio. Then, somehow or another, I took the notion that it would be advantageous to finish my higher education at an institution known all over the country. Ah! The Ohio State University—yep, that would do it. So, off I went to Columbus to make my case at the administration building on the prestigious campus of The Ohio State University.

Uh-oh. Things are not always as simple as they seem. The counselor noted that I was from out of state and proceeded to inform me that too many of their out-of-state graduates received degrees from the University, only to leave Ohio and work in other states—hence their policy to favor Ohio residents for matriculation approval. The counselor then threatened to put me on a lengthy waiting list.

Shucks, I knew there had to be some way around this policy. I told the counselor I was already a resident of Cleveland Heights and was looking over some properties so I could settle there. Bingo! That did it. I was taken in (and so was he).

The truth is, if you drive around Cleveland, you're bound to look over a lot of property. And, if some big company offered me a good job after graduation, I would certainly consider settling there—that part was true. Try putting that over on an admissions officer today!

I filled out an application and was accepted to OSU. A few months later, I saw a large poster hanging on the wall of the school cafeteria where I worked part-time. The word "Actors" written all over it in bold type caught my eye. The poster was a plea for student's voices to star in WOSU's radio dramas.

Hot spit! I was a student and I had a voice. And besides those two basic assets, I was a big ham: joking, clowning, and acting came naturally to me. Having treaded the boards several times at the Community Players Theatre in Huntington while I was at Marshall College, I had realized early on that I was a frustrated would-be actor with dreams of Hollywood stardom. Like thousands of other movie-actor wannabes, I knew my chances of making it big in show business were slim to none.

At the auditions, which were held at the WOSU radio studio, the staff handed me some scripts so I could prepare myself. I didn't think I had much of a shot because of my southern hick accent—maybe they'd let me play the village idiot. But I took a chance and did my best to knock off the Southern twang. To my surprise, I was handed the part of a Yankee general, while some Ohioan landed the Southern general's role. Ta-da!

During my last year at OSU, lots of radio acting roles came my way, and my appetite for performing grew. After graduation I bummed around for a couple of years in Detroit, working as a collections manager, but eventually I moved back to Huntington, West Virginia. With only a dabbler's background in radio, I dared to apply for an announcer's job at the local station, WPLH Radio. Hard up they must have been, because they hired me on the spot as a disc jockey and newscaster. "Wow! This is the big time!" I thought. "My first real broadcasting position!"

That was basically how I managed to get started in show business in the early 1950s. My Bachelor of Science degree in Business Administration had nothing to do with my career goals. Television was relatively new back in the 1950s, but even then you couldn't just walk into the local TV station, say you wanted to be a newscaster or sportscaster, and think they would give you an audition. You had to know someone who knew someone who could recommend your talent. And today, trying to break into the entertainment business is even more complicated. You'd first need a degree in communications before you could get through the door. Once inside, you'd start at the bottom, working at a small local radio or TV station. Typically, the "talent" (using the term as a job category, not an assessment of skill) comes in as a reporter, becomes an anchor, works for a year or two, sends out tapes, then takes an offer from a larger market. Back in the '50s, it had a lot to do with

144

being in the right place at the right time with the right talent for the right job.

WPLH in Huntington was a classroom for me. I learned the basic ins and outs of the business while working in radio. Goofing up while on the air was inevitable; I had to learn when to correct myself and when to let it slide. One day, while I was reading a commercial about the fresh watermelons available at a local market, I accidentally called them "vine-*rape* watermelons." I hastily corrected myself and changed it to "vine-*ripe* watermelons."

The program director heard my flub and said wisely, "When you correct yourself, it draws attention to your mistake. The next time you make a mistake, just keep on going and the audience will think they heard it wrong." It was a good lesson I never forgot, so when I was doing a Heiner's Bread commercial and said "For the breast in bed" instead of "For the best in bread," I just kept rolling.

WPLH's biggest competitor in town was Station WSAZ-TV and Radio, situated on the third floor of a downtown office building. Its listeners and viewers hailed from the tri-state area of West Virginia, Ohio, and Kentucky. The studio was a high-ceilinged affair with the announcer's booth on the main floor and a control room in a glassed-in section at the top. Every local announcer wanted to work there. I knew a few of the employees, and one day someone suggested I apply for a job opening at WSAZ-TV. With stars in my eyes, I went for an audition and landed a spot as a radio announcer. Later on, I was promoted to co-host of a late-night disc jockey show called *The Stan and Sam Show*, which ran from 11:30 p.m. to 1:00 a.m. every night. The "Sam" was Sam Lynn, who was already a popular TV personality—the producers thought it would be better if I had a well-known sidekick to chat with between records.

Our audience loved the show, and Sam and I had a great time kidding around on the air and playing all the top tunes of the day. Sometimes we played novelty records, one of which was called "What It Was, Was Football." Andy Griffith fans will be familiar with this tale of a country bumpkin fresh off the farm who has just witnessed his first game of football. Seeing football for the first time was pretty bizarre to this rube with his backwoods mentality. As the monologue goes on, the wonder and hilarity of football as seen through Andy's virgin eyes becomes a comedic feast for the listener.

One night, after playing this always-popular record, Sam and I decided we'd just call Andy up and chat with him live on our show. To our amazement and delight, Andy Griffith answered his phone. Try doing that with a celebrity today! We had a spontaneous, funny, interesting interview, which greatly entertained our audience for the evening. And it was my first brush with fame—Andy was a *little* bit famous back then.

146

Because the radio show was being so well received by the listeners, management began to look at me as a possible personality for the TV side of the station. My first television gig was as a lowest-of-the-lowly staff announcer, reading live station IDs and commercials from a tiny announcer's booth during NBC network breaks. Today, all these ads and commercials are videotaped beforehand, but back then everything was done live, or "on the air," as we say in show business.

It was station break time one afternoon when I turned on the microphone to read the station ID and a twenty-second spot and found myself with no script! Forgetting about the open mike, I stepped out of the booth and yelled irritably up to the director in the control room, "Where the f___ is the script?"

During a break of the *Tea and Trumpets* program. Don Waggoner, Stan Sweet, Dean Sturm, and Shawkey Saba.

My potty-mouthed expostulation made the director's eyes go wide and his mouth gape. He gave me a throat-cutting sign with his finger across his Adam's apple.

Uh-oh. I realized too late what I had done, so I quickly stepped back into the booth and read an old script in my most serious, sonorous voice: "This is WSAZ television, Channel Three in Huntington, West Virginia. Start your day right by reading the *Herald Dispatch*." Great start, Sweet.

Thankfully, there were never any repercussions from that terrible faux pas, and I graduated to doing live on-camera commercials for the local Philco refrigerator dealer. No teleprompters in those early days; we just had to memorize the pitches. Sam Lynn took his turn, and at the next break in network programming, I'd do mine. All went pretty well until one day they forgot to give me a "stand by" cue and the camera caught me picking my nose. That gaffe also went unmentioned—and when, during a pitch, I used the middle finger of my right hand to point out a feature on a Philco TV set, I still wasn't fired.

Local TV stations were always looking to fill in the air time that major networks hadn't bought. One day I came up with an idea for an afternoon musical program called "Tea and Trumpets." A fellow staffer by the name of Dean Sturm and I hosted the show by playing popular music over video footage. We'd also invite local singing or dancing teams to perform on our little get-together, down-home-and-cozy format.

The program went along smoothly and ratings were good, but the stars in my eyes got bigger and I decided to head for Hollywood, where I felt sure I could find real fame and fortune.

No brass bands awaited me when I pulled into Los Angeles, but my cousin Peggy Ford Gray met me and put me up for a few weeks in her San Fernando Valley home. Her husband, Phil Gray, was a popular vocalist on the *Spade Cooley Musical Hour*, a local weekly television program. Thanks to Peggy and Phil, I had a temporary headquarters until I found a job with Parkway Ford in Pasadena as a car and truck salesman.

The dealership managers thought that, with all my TV experience, I'd fare well as their TV spokesman doing live commercials for the Hollywood area. My TV spots brought a lot of business to the dealership, and from this exposure came offers to represent other businesses trying to increase their sales of trucks, campers, mobile homes, and cigarettes. It wasn't exactly the fame I was looking for, but it was a good start in a tough business in a tough town.

PART FOUR:
ODDBALL BITS AND PIECES

Chapter 1: Inventions We Need

There are a few inventions I'd like to see developed, even if they are a bit specialized.

How about something practical to hold your shirttail neatly under your belt—not Sansa Belt, Velcro, or a bodysuit, but something that doesn't require a lot of fuss?

How about a sprinkler pipe frame in your driveway to rinse off your car? It would consist of a large frame made of water pipes that have lots of holes drilled in them to spurt water all over your car. The water would stream downward and from the back, front, and sides for one or two minutes each time you came home. Just pull into the driveway, leave your car, push a button, and it will wash your car down after you've picked up dust, road grime, and mud from your recent drive. Fresh dirt comes off easily, so it would be a long time before you'd need it washed properly.

How about an exercise machine that's also an electric generator? Whether you're pedaling, pulling, or walking, it could generate current—not just to power your TV set, but to store in batteries that could cut in now and then, sending juice to your main house junction box. It would disconnect your outside source of power for a time while it furnished electricity for all your household needs. Your power company would not approve!

How about a STOL (short takeoff and landing) plane with lots of little extra wings that could be pumped out along the fuselage to create extra lift, allowing for a slower flight? Why, you could land or take off from the length of a football field, then retract the shortie wings into a smooth surface for faster, level flight. Hydraulics could produce the pressure to extend these short wings and a vacuum could retract them. Don't they already have these or some form thereof?

Back in 1959 I noticed that my Volkswagen Beetle had a reserve system for its gas tank. If you were forgetful and ran out of gas, you turned a lever and it started drawing gasoline from the bottom bulb of the tank. I thought it was a clever idea, so I installed that system on the regular flat tank of my 1964 Chevy Corvair.

Instead of having just the one pickup pipe running to the bottom of the gas tank, I opened the top of the tank, took out the factory feed line, and put another one alongside it, only about two inches shorter. The short one became the main source of fuel and the long one the reserve.

A two-way valve with an extension rod went up right under the dashboard, and the rod was bent ninety degrees for a two-inch control. Voila! My own "Reserve-a-gal" salvation, if I chanced to run out of go-juice. I tested it and found that the car could go another fifty miles on the reserve. I wish they had that feature on every car.

Here's an idea that I wish some progressive gun manufacturer would investigate and produce: a really flat .22 magnum semi-automatic pistol made of titanium, steel, and polyurethane. At less than an inch thick, it would be so skinny and light that it would be no trouble at all to conceal comfortably under your belt. With as small a caliber as a .22, it would be a dandy feat to produce such a low-profile weapon with plenty of stopping power. Off-duty policemen would glom onto it in a heartbeat. It wouldn't be much fun to shoot at the range, but it would come in handy for defense.

About forty years ago I was toying with two magnets and noticed how strong the resistance was when I tried to put the north pole of one against the north pole of the other one. Watching them repel each other gave me an idea. What if magnets ran along the bottom of your big rig set to aim downward with a north-pole impulse, and the road up a very steep hill had layers of north-pole impulses? If it were powerful enough, it would lighten your load, and climbing the hill would be a breeze. It wasn't practical at the time, but offered something to think about for future possibilities.

A few years later, lo and behold, when I was visiting a science exhibition at Disney World in Florida, I saw a display based on a nearly identical idea. I guess I wasn't crazy, after all. Certainly other applications of this same principle exist—for example, those overhead people movers that circulate through theme parks. And I'm sure there are other applications I don't know about in which magnetic forces can lighten loads.

Earlier I mentioned the sports and variety TV show that my friend Alton Tabor and I produced and hosted. We bought the air time for just a few hundred dollars on Sundays at KTTV Channel 11 and sold sponsorships to car dealers, mobile home dealers, and other businesses. (Those were the days when Earl Shibe in Hollywood advertised on TV, "I'll paint any car any color for $29.95.")

We interviewed people who had film of their sport or activity, such as river busting, skydiving, fast-draw demonstrations, weird inventions, and the like. One fellow had some film of a new flying machine, a small one-man helicopter that made power via hydrogen peroxide jets that passed through silver screens to the overhead prop blades. You see, pressing the hydrogen peroxide through the silver screens made it react violently and spew from the trailing edges of the copter blades to produce thrust, like a jet engine. The copter's little two-gallon fuel tank gave him almost an hour's flying time. The film demonstrated the machine's speed: it outraced a Ford Thunderbird over a one-mile course. The pilot's feet rested on a foot bar when he was airborne, and he landed on his own two feet when the flight was over.

Sometimes I wish I had a system of placards to show other motorists when they have an unknown problem and need to be advised. When they have a dragging tailpipe or a low tire or something hanging out of a door, you could tell them when you pass them. "LOW TIRE" one would say; "TAILPIPE LOW" another would say; "FLUID LEAKING" yet another; "YOU NERD!" for a careless driver, and so on. This idea is free for the taking, but if you start printing these cards, be sure you cut me in on the action by sending a set for my car.

While we're at it, I wish the state police or highway patrol had rear window signs to let us know as we pass why they stopped another motorist. Signs like "SPEEDING" or "BANK ROBBER" or "DRUG SUSPECT" or "DRUNK DRIVER" or "EXPIRED LICENSE" would be really helpful and might prevent rubbernecking. Yes, yes, I know. It's not practical, but it *would* be nice to know.

This is not an invention—just an idea I've had a lot of success with over the years. Some folks know about it, but most don't. I call it *The Bright Light Solution.* It's when you're almost ready to sneeze, but it won't quite finish—you're saying the "Ah, ah, ah," but the "*Choo!*" won't come. But if the sun is out or there's a bright light to look at, you can open your eyes wide and glance quickly at the light, and it will trigger the sneeze the rest of the way. I can get seven sneezes from this system most of the time, and very occasionally eight.

When I tell the average person about this technique, he or she looks at me as if I were wearing a green wig. The only scientific backing I can see for it is that it's a photoelectric process. All I say to the scoffers is, wait until one of these days when you have a sneeze just hanging there and you're afraid you'll lose a good one, glance at a bright light, and see what happens. Then join the B.L.S.A. (Bright-Light Sneezers of America).

Here's an inventive idea that you'd think would already be in play all over the country. Some enterprising person should buy a mobile snowmaking machine and go around making it look like a white Christmas when it's too warm even to entertain such a thought. You know the kind—the type the ski lodges use when it won't snow on its own. These things really pump out the snow. In just a couple of minutes your yard could have two inches of the white stuff on the lawn and bushes. Some fellows in Wisconsin are charging $250 to do this. (They should just charge a nominal fee like $50; they'd get a lot more business.) If it's not too warm, it would last several days. From Thanksgiving through New Year's Day, folks have their relatives coming to visit and would pay to brighten up their yards to impress the guests. You could just rent your machine to the ski lodges during their busiest times (except for Christmas). There's no charge for this idea, either, but I do ask that you do my yard for free every Christmas Eve. Who knows? You may have to buy two machines to keep up with the demand, especially if you can think of more uses for them.

Okay, here's another idea that needs some serious attention. You've heard of the "Dial a Prayer" campaign, haven't you? How about dialing for a compliment? Say you're just low in spirits. Or you've been called what you are and it hurts. Maybe you lost a deal or a job, or your wife or husband has tumbled onto your sneaky ways. *You need help.*

For 95 cents a minute, you could call "Dial a Smile" (a 900 number) to hear things like, "You're such a wonderful human being. Someday the whole world will know how great you really are. You are truly sensitive and, with the proper incentive, you're a workhorse." It would go on like this, pumping up your deflated ego. Then, at the end of the three minutes, a soothing voice would say, "Now take a deep breath, put a smile on your face, and think to yourself, 'I'm too good for this job and these thankless people, but I'll grin and bear it because they need me.'"

Let's wind up with a couple of my verbal inventions, ideas a couple of businesses could use. One is for a toupee maker's front sign: "GONE TODAY; HAIR TOMORROW." For J.C. Penney: "J.C. PANTIES, HALF OFF." The ad could show that cute little girl from the Coppertone sunblock ad where a dog is pulling her bathing suit down—"half off"—and revealing her bottom.

It's just a wild idea. J.C. Penney would never steal Coppertone's thunder like that, but it could create its own loveable cartoon character.

Chapter 2: The Stun Gun

Let's talk about the mysterious stun gun, a fascinating little gadget, akin to the much longer cattle prod, that takes a nine-volt battery and induces its power through a coil to increase its voltage thousands and thousands of times, so that it releases 50,000 to 400,000 volts or more at its tip. The device is meant to shock a person or animal into  submission temporarily, without permanent harm or damage, as a means of self-defense (or aggression).

It was in 1988 that I first heard more than a passing word about the different uses of these gizmos, which even then were no larger than two packs of cigarettes stacked atop one another. Local gun specialist Marvin Snedegar of Mountaineer Guns showed me an article that appeared in the June issue of *Outdoor Life Magazine*, reporting how doctors in Texas were using stun guns to lessen the trauma of rattlesnake bites for humans and dogs. (I know the idea sounds crazy, but so many documented cases made it hard to ignore.) One doctor had discovered that allowing the static-producing sparks that moved from one electrode to the other at the tip end of the stun gun to permeate the area of skin punctured by fang marks would dramatically reduce the terrible swelling that normally accompanied such an attack. (The victim, no doubt, would have to be held down to administer the shocks.) The scientific explanation was that the electrical shock alters the ionization of the venom's trace metal molecules so that they cannot attach themselves to animal tissue and destroy it, thereby reducing the trauma to the unlucky victim. It doesn't sound like much fun to be zapped for several seconds like that, but it's nothing compared to the pain and suffering of a poisonous snakebite. Obviously, care would have to be taken so that the victim didn't fall over or otherwise hurt himself during the stunning.

They had proved over and over again that the technique was safe and effective and kept records of all the cases, both those performed out in the desert and at the doctor's office. In a couple of cases, an automobile sparkplug wire was used to accomplish the same results when no one had a stun gun and the party was too far from town to seek medical help.

Stun guns are not normally used to kill or maim a human or animal; in most instances, they serve only as self-protection. They *can* be used for other than noble purposes, but we'll stay with self-protection. Take, for example, a big, burly guy who grabs a lady in the park or parking garage. She presses the electrodes hard up against his belly and jolts him with 50,000 volts or more, holding it tightly there until he drops helplessly to the ground.

I'm reminded of another usage for the stun gun, which I discovered accidentally when I went to visit some folks and parked in front of their house. I was about to open the car door when I encountered a huge mastiff growling and baring his teeth at me just a couple of feet away. I reached under the driver's seat, grabbed the stun gun, stuck it out the window, and let the thing crackle and spark in the dog's direction so he could hear and see those 50,000 volts in action. That's all it took. He backed off and kept his distance as I walked up the sidewalk to the house, crackling it now and then. It scared him away, and neither one of us got hurt in the process.

A stun gun is also a good thing to have if you jog or walk through lonely streets, or if you're a postman. My wife carries one with her as she walks our little twenty-three-pound Benji-type terrier-poodle mix. If a larger, aggressive canine tries to attack our friendly little pooch, she turns on the stun gun and crackles it to scare him away. If he bites our dog, she knows to jam the points of it into his rear and hold it there till he wilts to the ground. (Personally, I carry a tiny .22 revolver in my pocket when I walk the dog. With a black-powder blank cartridge up first in the cylinder, I'll give an attacking mongrel a black-powder enema to discourage his animosity.)

I bought a stun gun a few years ago for $29.95 that packs a 100,000-volt wallop, but you can pay up to $175.00 or more depending on the size, power, and brand. They're frequently available at gun shops, even if they aren't really bullet-shooting guns.

Chapter 3: Quickie Poems

As much as I like Robert Service's "The Cremation of Sam McGee," we won't go into any lengthy poetry today—just shorties that establish their point and then skedaddle before you know it. Pardon me if the wording is occasionally a little off from the way you knew it, but it should be close enough for government work. Some of these I'm sure you've heard or read before, and some you might not have. Some you'll like and some you won't. At any rate, they won't be long enough to bore you to tears.

I think it was Ogden Nash who wrote:

> *"Shake and shake the ketchup bottle;*
> *None will come and then a lot'll."*

Another of Ogden's goofy ones:

> *"The panther is like a leopard,*
> *Except hasn't been peppered.*
> *Should you behold a panther crouch,*
> *Prepare to say 'Ouch.'*
> *Better yet, if called by a panther,*
> *Don't anther."*

This two-liner I wrote to my wife:

> *"Do you love me or do you not?*
> *You told me once, but I forgot."*

A quote from an egotist:

> *"I love me. I think I'm grand.*
> *I go to the movies just to hold my hand."*

This one's a poetic puzzle. See if you can guess the answer:

> *"A man without eyes saw plums on a tree.*
> *He neither took plums, nor left plums.*
> *Now, how could that be?"*

It's really not impossible. Just think on it. Try to figure it out before you read the answer. I've typed it backwards, so there won't be any temptation to look before you think. (.plums two the of one took and eye one only had He)

L.A. disc jockey Dick Whittinghill gave us this one on the air:

> *"I kissed the brown-eyed cow that gives us milk and*
> *cheese.*
> *I'm in the clinic now, with hoof-and-mouth disease."*

I'm not positive, but I think D.O. Flynn wrote this one:

> *"Though very swift is an eyelid's flicker,*
> *A grapefruit's squirt is even quicker."*

I don't know what came over someone to corrupt this oldie:

"Thirty days hath September, April, June, and November. All the rest have peanut butter, except me and I ride a bicycle."

When I was in the service we would see written on the walls everywhere, "KILROY WAS HERE FIRST." Sometimes, along with Kilroy's boastful message, there was even a crude drawing of a long-nosed character looking over a fence. It always said, "SMOE SEES YOU." Don't ask me why, but Smoe and Kilroy certainly got around in those days.

One day I was in the john and saw where a guy had happily scrawled:

"TODAY MY HEART IS FILLED WITH JOY, FOR I WAS HERE BEFORE KILROY."

Then, the *very next day,* some dude had written under that inscription:

"SORRY TO SPOIL YOUR LITTLE JOKE. I WAS HERE FIRST, BUT MY PENCIL BROKE." (signed) KILROY

Bathrooms were loaded with graffiti, some clever, some poetic:

"YOU'D CERTAINLY THINK FROM ALL THIS WIT,
THAT SHAKESPEARE'S GHOST HAD COME TO
_____."

Or:

"BE LIKE DAD, NOT LIKE SIS.
LIFT THE LID TO TAKE A _____."

In the vestibule of the Air Corps mess hall, there was a poster warning of venereal disease. A beautiful gal gazed out at us, and underneath her picture it said, "She may *look* clean, but . . ."

Then, just below that message, some guy had printed,

"IF SHE'S GOT IT, I WANT IT."

This goofy one was entitled "A Sunday Morn":

"As I awoke this morning, when sweet things are born,
A robin perched upon my sill to signal the coming morn.
The bird was fragile, young, and gay
so sweetly did it sing,
That thoughts of happiness and joy
into my heart did spring.
It hummed softly with a cheery song. Then, as it paused
for a moment's lull,
I gently closed the window and crushed its f---ing skull."

To the tune of "My Bonnie Lies Over the Ocean," here's a variation:

> *"My Bonnie leaned over the gas tank,*
> *The contents she did want to see.*
> *She lit a match in her excitement.*
> *Bring back my poor Bonnie to me."*

There is an old song by Eben E. Rexford that begins, "Darling, I am growing old, silver threads among the gold." Some wiseacre changed the words to accommodate this version:

> *"In the boarding house where I stayed,*
> *Everything was growing old.*
> *Silver hairs among the butter,*
> *And the bread had turned to mold.*
> *When the dog died we had sausage,*
> *Cat died we had catnip tea.*
> *When the landlord died, I left there.*
> *Spareribs were too much for me."*

Wanda Cunningham's quickie, called "Heaven Forbid!":

> *"I hope that I shall never see*
> *A dog who thinks that I'm a tree!"*

A short and gory one of unknown origin:

> *"He tried to cross the railroad track*
> *Before the rushing train.*
> *They put the pieces in a sack,*
> *But couldn't find the brain."*

Joey Russell, in *Parade Magazine*, wrote this one about educating kids:

> *"My daughter has her master's,*
> *My son his Ph.D.,*
> *But Father is the only one*
> *Who has a J.O.B."*

Remember this one in case you're accused of bragging:

> *"A man should blow his own big horn.*
> *This right should not be mooted.*
> *For, if he does not blow his horn,*
> *The same will not be tooted."*

A silly one by the late Samantha Brown, who was quite a poetess:

> *"All the world loves a lover.*
> *Declare your love before the world.*
> *Sing love songs o'er its clamor,*
> *Hug and kiss each one you meet,*
> *And they'll put you in the slammer."*

Another of Samantha's:

> *"Early to bed, early to rise,*
> *And all you get are dark, baggy eyes."*

Samantha wrote this one, too:

> *"My lover loves discreetly;*
> *Wisely, if not well;*
> *Thus, he loves me seldom.*
> *I hope he rots in hell."*

Here's one I found in a grade school book when I was a kid:

> *"Do not steal this book, my lad,*
> *For fifty cents it cost my dad.*
> *'Cause if you do, the Lord will say:*
> *"Where's that book you stole one day?"*
> *And you will say, "I don't know."*
> *And the Lord will say, "To hell you go."*

Women versus men—you've heard this one before:

> *"Women have many faults,*
> *Men have but two.*
> *Everything they say,*
> *And everything they do."*

On safe gun handling:

> *"Never, never let your gun*
> *Pointed be at anyone.*
> *That it should unloaded be,*
> *Matters not the least to me."*

After an accidental burp:

> *"Pardon me for being so rude.*
> *It wasn't me; it was the food.*
> *It got lonely down below.*
> *It just came up to say hello."*

Or an alternate ending:

> *"It got lonely way down there.*
> *It just came up for a breath of air."*

Who wrote this one? It sure sounds like Armour or Nash:

> *"The bee is a simple soul,*
> *And not concerned with birth control.*
> *Which explains, in times like these,*
> *You see so many sons of bees."*

"Sprig Poeb" (Spring Poem)—from someone with a really stuffed-up nose:

"By dose is dribblig,
By eyes are red.
I wush thad I was hobe in bed.
I've used all dose drops by head cad hode,
But still I've got this dabbed old code."

And, finally, Richard Armour on the shallowness of bathtubs:

"No singer in bathtubs, I lift up my voice
Against a contraption that gives me the choice
Of sitting bolt upright and warming my knees,
While my chest and my back and my upper parts freeze,
Or dunking the top of me, forepart and aft,
And exposing my legs and my feet to the draft.
In short, I'm too long and I can't for the soul of me
Submerge, as I'd like, at one moment the whole of me.
So, I shift back and forth and unhappily fidget,
And swear that the tub was designed by a midget."

My, but those were refreshingly short, weren't they?

Chapter 4: Malapropisms and New Words

The famous Mrs. Malaprop is a very confused character in the 1775 play *The Rivals* by Richard Brinsley Sheridan. She substituted wrong words that sounded something like the proper ones. Her gaffes were funny to those who knew the difference—for example, "He is the very pineapple of politeness." Sheridan coined the name Malaprop, which came from the French *mal* ("bad") and *à propos* ("to the purpose" or "fitting"), thus meaning "inappropriate." Let's check into some of the ones I've heard. Maybe you've heard them, too.

With his bad kidneys, they put him on a "dye alice" machine. (Instead of "dialysis")

He had a "corollary thumbosis."
(Instead of "coronary thrombosis")

She had a lot of personal "maggotism."
(Instead of "magnetism")

It was "unconscional" behavior.
(Instead of "unconscionable")

Arte Johnson of Laugh-In used to say, "It's 'unbelievigable!'"
(Instead of "unbelievable")

Jimmy Durante used to say, "It's a 'catastroscope.'"
(Instead of "catastrophe")

She was having her "administration" period.
(Instead of "menstruation")

He was suffering "defusions of grander."
(Instead of delusions of grandeur)

I "gonorrhea" you one thing, it's "invenereal" to me.
(Instead of "guarantee" and "immaterial")

If you don't see your favorite malapropism here, don't get "historical." You could get nervous "prostitution."

The Ultimate Political Speech!

Closely akin to a malapropism is this short speech by an unknown author. He uses big words in such a way that it makes his opponent sound bad, even though he's really saying nice things about the man. See how cleverly he's worded the speech—I had to look up some of the words myself. It goes like this:

"My fellow citizens, it is an honor and a pleasure to be here today. My opponent has openly admitted that he feels an affinity toward our city, but I happen to like this area. It might be a salubrious place to him, but to me it is one of the nation's most delightful garden spots.

"When I embarked upon this political campaign, I had hoped that it could be conducted on a high level and that my opponent would be willing to stick to the issues. Unfortunately, he has decided to be tractable, instead—to indulge in unequivocal language, to eschew the use of outright lies in his speeches, and even to make repeated veracious statements about me.

170

"At first I tried to ignore these scrupulous, unvarnished fidelities. Now I will do so no longer. If my opponent wants a fight, he's going to get one!

"It might be instructive to start with his background. My friends, have you ever accidentally dislodged a rock on the ground and seen what was underneath? Well, exploring my opponent's background is quite dissimilar. All the slime and filth and corruption you can possibly imagine, even in your wildest dreams, are glaringly nonexistent in this man's life—even during his childhood!

"Let us take a very quick look at that childhood. It is a known fact that, on a number of occasions, he emulated older boys at a certain playground. It is also known that his parents not only permitted him to masticate excessively in their presence, but even urged him to do so. Most explicable of all, this man, who poses as a paragon of virtue, exacerbated his own sister when they were both teenagers!

"I ask you, my fellow Americans, is this the kind of person we want in public office to set an example for our youth?

"Of course, it's not surprising that he should have such a typically pristine background—no, not when you consider the other members of his family.

"His female relatives put on a constant pose of purity and innocence and claim they are inscrutable, yet every one of them has taken part in hortatory activities.

171

"The men are, likewise, completely amenable to moral suasion. My opponent's second cousin indulges in interdigitation. His uncle was a flagrant heterosexual.

"His sister, who has always been obsessed by sects, once worked as a proselyte outside a church.

"His father was secretly chagrined at least a dozen times by matters of a pecuniary nature.

"His youngest brother wrote an essay extolling the virtues of being a *homo sapiens*.

"His nephew subscribes to a phonographic magazine.

"His great aunt expired from a degenerative disease.

"His wife was a thespian before their marriage and even performed the act in front of paying customers.

"And his own mother had to resign from a woman's organization in her later years because she was an admitted sexagenarian.

"Now, what can I say of the man, himself? I can tell you in solemn truth that he is the very antithesis of political radicalism, economic irresponsibility, and personal depravity. His own record proves that he has frequently discountenanced treasonable, un-American philosophies and has perpetrated many overt acts, as well.

"He perambulated his own infant son on the street.

"He practiced nepotism with his uncle and first cousin.

"He attempted to interest a thirteen-year-old girl in philately.

"He participated in a séance at a private residence where, among other odd goings-on, there was incense.

"He has declared himself in favor of more homogeneity on college campuses.

"He has advocated social intercourse in mixed company—and has taken part in such gatherings himself.

"He has been deliberately averse to crime in our city streets.

"He has urged our Protestant and Jewish citizens to develop more catholic tastes.

"Last summer he committed a piscatorial act on a boat that was flying the American flag.

"Finally, at a time when we must be on our guard against all foreignisms, he has coolly announced his belief in altruism and his fervent hope that, some day, this entire nation will be altruistic!

"I beg you, my friends, to oppose this man, whose life and work and ideas are so openly and avowedly compatible with our American way of life. A vote for

173

him would be a vote for the perpetuation of everything we hold dear.

"The facts are clear; the record speaks for itself. Do your duty."

New Words

Right along with malapropisms are new words that are not yet in the dictionary, but may have a right to be there someday. Some of these you've heard before and some I've hatched up myself.

There is *succinctify*, which means "to condense"; *oxtigate*, which means "to separate the B.S. from the truth," which you do subconsciously when you know someone is exaggerating or embellishing the truth; *inhumid*, which means "dry;" and *academia nuts*, which are college professors and the like who are monomaniacs about language or some other subject.

Here's a phrase you can use to describe a phony medical problem when it's too personal to disclose the truth to a nosy person: "I have 'diphlucous of the left clavicle,' sometimes misdiagnosed as *proctalgia fugax*."

A "purse closenal" friend describes somebody helping you who has a lot of money. *Nostrilia* is nostril cilia, or ugly nose hair, in abundance. *Sacrifasting* is sacrificing by denying yourself food during Lent. *Prissy footing* is pussyfooting in a prissy way. A *motorologist* is a well-schooled mechanic. *Penistration* is my new medical term that means penetration with you-know-what. *Absotively* and *posilutely*, which are spoonerisms of "absolutely"

174

and "positively," just make you sound cool. Then there are three combination words that denote either or both sexes or someone of unknown sex: *his/her* (pronounced "hizzer"), *him/her* (pronouced "himmer"), and *he/she* (pronounced "hishee"). Lastly, there is *mediocritizing*, which someone coined to mean doing things in a mediocre way instead of trying for the best.

Overheard in a doctor's office: "I just can't quit smoking, Doc."

"Oh, yes, you can, sir." Can, sir. Cancer.

Feel free to utilize these new words and ideas in your own daily conversations and writings whenever you so desire.

Chapter 5: Pet Peeves

Now back to people, and things that bug me and probably irritate you, too. Let's just list them one right after the other.

Very slow drivers on crooked two-lane roads who hold up several vehicles behind them. (Cops in California will give you a ticket, if you are holding up five or more vehicles—and they can get to you.)

How about people with little yapping dogs that they can't or won't shut up?

People who pee on commode seats and leave it for you to see or sit on.

Those who splatter even worse stuff and don't clean it off before they leave.

People with dangerous dogs.

People with loud or unruly kids.

"Snags" (things that get in your way and hold you up when you want to go somewhere or get something done).

People who borrow your stuff and don't bring it back.

People on the highway who decide to do some passing of their own while you're passing *them*.

People ahead of you who drive too slowly in the snow, making you lose momentum and thus forcing you to start slipping so that you can't move up the hill.

Line buckers—people who pop into a line ahead of you, so they don't have to wait like you do.

Paranoiacs or bigots of any race—especially the aggressive ones.

Movies that spend too much time on oppression.

Movies that never show the oppressors getting their comeuppance.

People in the fastest freeway lane who are going slower than all the other traffic and won't move over when you loom up in their rearview mirrors, or even when you flash your lights.

People who slurp loudly while they're eating and don't get it when you say, "I hear you like that."

People who wear shirts or blouses more than once without checking to see whether they smell of B.O. Not to mention those who don't use deodorant or don't bathe, and the like.

People who jump to a negative conclusion when a tiny shred of doubt lands on someone. The aggressive ones are the worst.

How about guys (usually four of them) who go into bars and say, "This one's on me, fellas" (playing the big shot). Then each one taking his turn being the wheel (you might hear "Your money's no good") and getting angry if one of them wants to leave before standing the others to a round. Just pay your own way each time and say you may have to leave early, instead of playing Mr. Macho.

People who purposely break wind in the presence of others.

Clerks who act like they own the place and refer to "my inventory," or who don't get up to look for something and simply tell you they don't have it, when you know they did just an hour ago.

Government clerks who act tough because they know you need their services and can't get them anywhere else—especially the ones who push weak people around or use petty, mean little delaying tactics if you don't show them obeisance.

People who leave their TVs or radios on high volume while you're trying to talk with them for a few moments.

People who wear shorts when they have horrible-looking legs or are extremely obese.

Holes in the toe of your sock where the big toe sticks out and hangs up.

Men's briefs (shorts) that are way too large in the legs and don't contain you properly.

Bras that allow part of the breast to slide out.

Vacuum cleaners that won't pick up something unless you feed it to them.

Dishwashers that won't clean well unless you pre-wash each soiled item.

How about people who pull out onto a highway from their driveways with no regard to the flow of traffic, then piddle along at 25 mph, holding you up? I pulled out of my mother's driveway one day; at the highway's edge was a big, bushy hedge, blocking my view of traffic from the left. I tried to see through the cracks, but couldn't see anything moving, so I pulled out in front of some guy, who screeched to a stop to keep from hitting me. I gulped, drove on down to the next stoplight, and stopped in the right lane to wait for the green light. Meanwhile, this irate fellow pulled up on my left side and stopped, looking my way to see what a true idiot looked like. I cooperated by turning his way, crossing my eyes and twisting my mouth with my tongue hanging out, looking like I didn't have a brain in my head. He broke up and laughed, and so did I. No sense disappointing people, is there? I would have been mad if he had done it to me.

You know what else burns my butt? A flame about that high.

Chapter 6: Wrongs That Need a-Rightin'

Sadly enough, some businesspeople don't feel obligated to live up to their promises in providing services for money paid or work done. I recently read Ron Burley's article in the March/April 2007 issue of *AARP Magazine* about the necessity of insisting that careless or conniving folks come through with what they promise.

Burley demonstrated to the manager of a tire store how he could (and would) put a few dents in their future sales if they didn't make good on his demands for proper recompense. That's all it took. He got full restitution on the deal that had hoodwinked his wife into buying "el cheapo" tires, even though she had already driven them home.

The article reminded me of the time my son appeared on the TV program *The Dating Game* in September of 1979. He won an all-expenses-paid trip to Europe. They piddled around and stalled for a whole year, and would not send the tickets or expense money to him or the young lady who also won and was to accompany him. Nor would they send them a check for the agreed value of the trip.

It was time, I calculated, to sit down and knock out a letter to these recalcitrant, arrogant bigshots who were taking advantage of innocent participants on their popular program. I composed the two letters following to see if I could shake something loose from these birds.

The first was sent to the emcee and the producers of the show and was mailed to them in September of 1980.

To Whom It May Concern:

My son, Jody Alan Sweet, won a trip to Amsterdam from you folks a year ago. The trip, you said, was valued at $1,465.00, but to date no one has arranged for his trip or sent him the cash it represented.

Would you please let me have the name and address of someone who would be responsible for making good on this, so that my Los Angeles attorney or David Horowitz can contact him or her for some kind of quick, positive action?

I'm sure that people like Geraldo Rivera, Mike Wallace, or my friend at *The National Enquirer* would not be interested in investigating until we have tried at least one more time to get some proper results.

Hoping to hear from you within the next couple of weeks.

(I signed it with my complete address and had copies go to emcee Chuck Barris and my son.)

Nine months later we had not received any redress in the matter, so I sat down once again and whipped out a letter, this time to *The National Enquirer*. I have no idea why we waited so long to get tough with these people who were obviously not willing to cough up what they owed and had promised. That missive, dated June 4, 1981, went like this:

Messrs. Gregor, Jenkins & Porter:

National Enquirer (Lantana, Florida)

Dear Sirs:

Perhaps you'll find something interesting here to investigate.

Going on two years ago now, my son, Jody A. Sweet, appeared on *The Dating Game Show* (Chuck Barris Production #A61-79), where they announced to the world that he had won an all-expenses-paid trip to Amsterdam, Holland. So far they've done nothing but double-talk the boy, and goodness knows how many others are in the same boat.

We realize that it was a trade deal they had made with the airlines, hotels, etc., and that the coordination required some effort, but they can't keep using that excuse. They've obviously deceived the public with their promises, and they even sent my son a W-2 tax form for $1,400 that they charged off last year—and we *know* that is illegal.

The juicy exposé potential of big businessmen who recently contemplated the purchase of a multimillion-dollar ball club and can't seem to honor a $1,400 commitment to a trusting young man, plus the probability of shaking a lot more out of this same tree, should interest some zealous reporter. I'm hoping that one of you will see to it that this is followed through on properly.

At any rate, if I don't hear anything within a couple weeks, I'll rewrite this letter and send it to another medium. Thanks a lot.

Stan Sweet

That one did the trick. Only a couple of days later, a staff member from *The National Enquirer* called from Florida, asking me to hold off on contacting others in the media—they were hot on the trail and working up an article for publication soon. To make sure my son and I had copies, they mailed us one within a week. This is a clipping of what they sent:

Well, a few days after that issue hit the streets Jody was sent a check for the $1,465. He invested it in musical sound equipment and later had two country & western hit songs in the top ten national ratings. One was Lari White's recording of "Ready, Willing, and Able," and the other was Trace Atkin's hit recording of "Lonely Won't Leave Me Alone."

As Ron Burley so aptly put it in his *AARP Magazine* article, "Sometimes you need to be a bully to get what you deserve."

PART FIVE: MORE COLORFUL CHARACTERS

Chapter 1: Gunmen

Along with my reputation as a shooter, I am also licensed to carry a concealed weapon, which I do, most of the time. If I'm in a state where they don't recognize 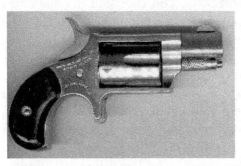 my gun permit, I can only say this: "I'd rather be caught with one than without one." At my advanced age, I do not feel obligated to suffer physical harm from some drugged-up knife wielder or some bruiser threatening to beat me. I reserve the right to defend myself, my family, and my property by any means at hand.

I've never had to use a gun in defense of my life against another human being, but I have had to resort to firing blank cartridges at dogs a few times. I've always known that if some large dog started chewing on my little twenty-three-pound terrier, I'd give him a loud burn across the butt.

One summer afternoon I had occasion to talk with my brother-in-law Freddie Giggenbach, who was operating a bulldozer and leveling some land. He was located at the end of a narrow lane on the outskirts of town, and I couldn't drive to where he was pushing the dirt around— I had to walk the last bit.

After parking the car, I looked down the bumpy lane and saw a huge Great Dane standing in the middle of the path as if he owned the place. I palmed my little North American .22 revolver and set out to see Freddie. As I walked down the way, the big dog growled at me. I loudly shooed him off with hopeful bravado. He didn't sound as if he were going to attack me, so I walked on past him, thinking he was all bluff.

But the dog sneaked up behind me quietly and grabbed my left elbow in his massive jaws, very lightly, just to show me that he was the boss. It scared me, so I fired a blank cartridge right under him. BAM! He took off running, and I figured that was the end of that naughty boy.

Freddie had stopped his dozer for a minute to answer my questions about improving some property, and, when we concluded our chat, I headed back up the narrow road. I looked around as I was walking back, to see if I could spot that big, horsey dog again. There he was, peering around the corner of a house, with just his head sticking past it. Apparently he'd had enough of me and my blazing, noisy gun.

On another occasion, it was a summer evening and I had my driver's-side window rolled down. I was driving up into the hills above Pasadena on an insurance call. As

I got near the house I was looking for, a tremendously loud bark hit my ears and scared the daylights out of me. A hundred-pound German Shepherd was running alongside my slow-moving vehicle, venting his pent-up venom so harshly that I swerved in reaction. "I'll fix him if he does that again on my way back," I thought.

After my interview, I pulled out my old .45 single-action Colt revolver from under the seat and started driving back down that little road along the canyon. Sure enough, here came that idiot monster to hassle me once more, barking loudly like a fool. I stuck the gun out the window and fired a big balloon-load black-powder blank right at his chest as I drove along slowly. He was just under my window, so the blast must have burned him smartly, because when I looked in the rearview mirror, he was stopped with his head down and shaking it off. Some people just don't go to the trouble of training their animals properly.

 Talking about those who don't train their animals, I recently had another occasion to be on the receiving end of this lack of basic animal training. Cujo, my little Benji-type terrier, and I walk a mile or two every day and a take a short walk every evening. We go up a dead-end street that leads to the twenty-five-acre spread of the National Fish Hatchery.

186

The folks who live in the last house on the left side of the street own a large black Chow/Alaskan Husky-mix dog that is usually fenced in. Although we've been walking on the opposite sidewalk past the place for over ten years, the dumb animal still barks its fool head off when we go by. You'd think that after all these thousands of trips the loud-mouthed canine would know we're not a threat and let us pass in peace.

Often, though, the gate is left open and the dog roams the neighborhood, much to my chagrin. One day this big female Alaskan sled-puller dog came roaring over from her side of the street to ours, teeth bared and growling loudly, heading straight for little Cujo. I quickly stepped into her path, stomped my foot, and yelled at her. She stopped and retreated a few feet to let us pass.

I told her owner about the incident and let him know that I would kill his dog if she ever bit me or Cujo. Instead of apologizing, he took the threat seriously. He's been civil but cool toward me ever since. "What does he expect me to do?" I wondered.

One dark evening not long afterwards, we were walking back from the Fish Hatchery. All of a sudden, out of the darkness we heard this horrible menacing growl. I jerked around in time to see this same monster moving toward us again, as if to attack. I stood my ground and yelled at her to get away. She wouldn't budge, so I pulled out my little pistol and fired a blank cartridge into the pavement right in front of her. She

187

dashed away that time, so we kept walking. I heard the front door of her owner's house open. A quick glance revealed silhouettes of people in the light, so I pocketed the gun and we went along our merry way as if nothing had happened. I wonder what they thought. I remembered the saying, "The careful application of terror is also a form of communication."

Since then, that dog gives us a wide berth when she's out, but still barks her dumb head off when she's penned up and we're passing.

While traveling the eleven western states with my comedy gun act in 1970, I chanced to run into another entertainer from our agency, who was touring with his hypnotism act. Jack Lithgow, his wife, and I decided to have dinner together that evening to chat about our bookings. He told me about the night before, when he had had to use *his* gun.

Jack and his wife had pulled into the parking lot of a motel and were leaving their vehicle to retire for the evening. They saw two large young men, one black and one white, standing along the walkway that led to their rooms. They didn't seem to fit in or belong there, so Jack picked up his book, clipboard, and Ruger .22 semi-automatic pistol, which he held underneath the clipboard, out of sight.

Jack was leading the way, his wife a few steps behind him on the sidewalk, when the two suspicious-looking young men started walking toward them. They nodded a friendly greeting to the fellows and carried on past them, when all at once he heard his wife scream. He whipped around just in time to see one of them holding her and at the same time felt the edge of a brick bounce off the side of his head, momentarily stunning him.

He almost fell, dropping his book and clipboard, but he clung onto the pistol. The two thugs saw the gun, let go of his wife, and took off running across the parking lot. He shook his head to clear his vision and shot at the running figure of the one who had hit him with the brick. The shot hit the guy in the thigh, but he limped away and vaulted over a fence after his buddy.

Jack reported the incident to the local police. Later the mugger checked into a hospital and was arrested. I commented on Jack's fine shooting—he had merely wounded the attacker instead of hitting a vital area. But Jack sidestepped the compliment. "'Fine shooting?' I was mad as hell and trying to kill that S.O.B.!"

I heard about a similar situation when I met an old schoolmate, Grover Burns, on the sidewalk in my West Virginia hometown. I had been living in California for thirty years and was glad to see someone I knew from the old days. Grover shook my hand when I told him that I had been gone for many years and was happy to be back. He mentioned that he was also happy to be back in town, because he had just been released from prison. I raised an eyebrow, and he explained that he had shot a guy with a shotgun during a fight.

"You just wounded the guy?" I asked.

"Yeah," he said. "I hit him in the shoulder."

189

"Good control," I complimented.

"Control, hell," he countered. "I meant to kill the bastard!"

Two tough ones in a row—thank goodness my problems only involved dogs and I never even had to use real bullets.

Chapter 2: Motorcycle Tire Repair

Just a couple of miles outside my hometown in southeastern West Virginia, I owned a big, old farmhouse, along with about thirty acres of hillside and just a few acres of bottom land. It was located right across the one-lane paved road from the Valley View Country Club golf course.

One summer day I got the notion that it would be nice to ride up to the top of the hill, where I had an apple orchard, and see what kind of view I had up there—the elevation was almost three thousand feet. I jumped on my trusty Honda motorcycle and low-geared it to the top, sat down to smoke a cigarette, made my observations, and decided to go back down the rain-gutted dirt road.

Uh-oh—the rear tire was as flat as a stomped-on hat. "Not to worry," I thought. I reached for the can of tire repair foam in the bag that sat alongside the frame of the machine, figuring I'd whip that sucker out and pump the tire back up, sealing the puncture at the same time. I'd had the can for two or three years and had never needed to use it, so I assumed it would still be full of that white, gooey stuff and compressed air.

I smiled smugly, removed the offending roofing nail from the tread of the tire, and screwed the tip of the can onto the valve stem so that it could shoot its contents into the sick casing. But it didn't. It just gave a short "whoosh" and nothing more–no sealing or pumping up the tire. I tried it a few times more, but to no avail.

I sighed wearily and started walking the heavy vehicle all the way down that rough road. It wanted to roll faster than I could walk, but I squeezed the hand brake to slow it down. I finally made it back to the farmhouse and parked the cycle. By this time I was furious. After carrying that "means of salvation" (so the can's labeling proclaimed) all those years and finding that it didn't even work, I had to have some satisfaction, or at least revenge.

I went into the house, grabbed my Colt .45 Commander semi-automatic pistol, and walked back to the motorcycle. I took the worthless can of white junk and threw it up the hill to use as a target. Backing up about thirty feet, I took dead aim and hit it on the first shot. POW! BOOM! The white goop exploded all over the place. But that didn't satisfy me, so I kept shooting the dumb thing over and over till I ran out of ammunition.

I stopped, letting the gun hang down by my side. Then I heard shouting over my shoulder.

"IS THAT IT?"

It was coming from the golf course about forty yards behind me.

When I turned around, I saw four men standing in the fairway, one of them with his golf club raised over his head. He was waiting for the noise to abate so he could concentrate on hitting the ball.

I bowed obsequiously and yelled back, "YEAH, THAT'S IT! SORRY."

Afterword

There you are, folks: a compilation of people, animals, and things that have caught my interest over my long life. My fast-draw days are over, but I still shoot Cowboy Action, where you draw slow and shoot fast. Nowadays I'm known as "Half-Fast Stanley" (don't say that quickly). Yes, these days I'm the *second* fastest gun in town, and I'm not looking for the first.

If you've learned anything new or bizarre, or have enjoyed insights about people and things that never occurred to you before, that's wonderful. I thank you for your kind attention.